Joseph Ritson

Ancient Popular Poetry - From Authentic Manuscripts and Old Printed Copies

Vol. I

Joseph Ritson

Ancient Popular Poetry - From Authentic Manuscripts and Old Printed Copies
Vol. I

ISBN/EAN: 9783337251093

Printed in Europe, USA, Canada, Australia, Japan

Cover: Foto ©Thomas Meinert / pixelio.de

More available books at **www.hansebooks.com**

COLLECTANEA ADAMANTÆA.—V.

Ancient Popular Poetry:
FROM
AUTHENTIC MANUSCRIPTS
AND
OLD PRINTED COPIES.

Edited by
JOSEPH RITSON,
AND
Revised by
EDMUND GOLDSMID, F.R.H.S.

ADORNED WITH CUTS

VOL. I.

PRIVATELY PRINTED.
EDINBURGH.
1884.

PREFACE.

THE genius which has been successfully exerted in contributing to the instruction or amusement of society, in even the rudest times, seems to have some claim upon its gratitude for protection in more enlightened ones. It is a superannuated domestic, whose passed services entitle his old age to a comfortable provision and retreat; or rather, indeed, a humble friend, whose attachment in adverse circumstances demands the warm and grateful acknowledgments of prosperity. The venerable though nameless bards whom the generosity of the public is now courted to rescue from oblivion and obscurity, have been the favourites of the people for ages, and could once boast a more numerous train of applauding admirers than the most celebrated of our modern poets. Their compositions, it may be true, will have few charms in the critical eye of a cultivated age; but it should always be remembered, that, without such efforts, humble as they are, cultivation or refinement would never exist, and barbarism and ignorance be eternal. It is to an ENNIUS, perhaps, that we are indebted for a VIRGIL, to such writers as PEELE and GREENE, or others still more obscure, that we owe the admirable dramas of our divinest SHAKSPEARE; and if we are ignorant of the comparatively wretched attempts which called forth the deservedly immortal powers of HOMER or CHAUCER, it is by no means to be infered that they were the earliest of poets, or sprung into the world, as has been said of the inimitable dramatist already mentioned, like Minerva out of the head of Jupiter, at full growth, and mature.

> *Vixere fortes ante Agamemnona*
> *Multi; sed omnes illacrymabiles*
> *Urgentur, ignotique longâ*
> *Nocte.*

Any enquiry, it is presumed, after the authors of these fugitive productions is at present impossible. It can only be conjectured that they were written (or, more accurately speaking, perhaps, imagined and committed to memory) by men, who made it their profession to chant or rehearse them, up and down the country, in the trophyed hall or before the gloomy castle, and at marriages, wakes and other festive meetings, and who generally accompanyed their strains, by no means ruder than the age itself, with the tinkling of a harp, or sometimes, it is apprehended, with the graces of a much humbler instrument. It may, indeed, be conceived that they would now and then be furnished with a superior performance from the cloister or college; as even the great sir Thomas More has left us something of the same kind [1]. But, however it was, they seem to have been more attentive to temporary applause or present emolument than to future fame, of which they had possibly no idea, and, while they consigned their effusions to the casual protection of an auditors memory, were totally indifferent whether they were remembered or forgotten. The consequence is that while we are indebted for those which remain to accident and good fortune, numbers have perished, not less, and possibly even more, worthy of preservation. The reader who wishes for further information concerning this set of men may find his curiosity gratified by consulting Dr. Percys very ingenious and elegant "Essay on the ancient English Minstrels," prefixed to his "*Reliques of ancient English Poetry*," and some "Observations" on the same character in a collection of "*Ancient Songs*," published by J. Johnson, in St. Pauls Church-yard [2].

---

[1] "A mery iest how a sergeaunt would learne to play the frere. Written in hys youth (for his pastime)." See his *Workes*, 1557, and the "History of the English language," prefixed to Dr. Johnsons *Dictionary*.

[2] It is suspected, however, that the present copy of the *History of Tom Thumb* has been modernised by some ballad-writer of Queen Elizabeths time; very probably the same Richard Johnson who afterward turned it into prose.

PREFACE.

It might naturally enough excite the surprise of the intelligent reader, that in a professed republication of popular poetry, nothing should occur upon a subject indisputably the most popular of all—the history of our renowned English archer, ROBIN HOOD. Some apology is undoubtedly necessary on this head, as the omission is by no means owing to ignorance or neglect. In fact, the poems, ballads, and historical or miscellaneous matter, in existence, relative to this celebrated outlaw, are sufficient to furnish the contents of even a couple of volumes considerably bulkyer than the present; and fully deserve to appear in a separate publication, "unmix'd with baser matter."[1]

It would be no trifling gratification to the editor of this little volume, and contribute in some degree, he is persuaded, to the amusement of even the literary part of the public, if the present attempt should be productive of others of a similar nature. Many of our old poems, which would even now be of acknowledged excellence, are scarcely known by name. Such, for instance, are "*The wife lapped in Morels skin, or The taming of a shrew,*" "*The high way to the spittle house,*" "*The schole house of women,*" "*The unlucky firmentie,*" and some others; all or most of which abound with a harmony, spirit, keenness, and natural humour, little to be expected, perhaps, in compositions of so remote a period, and which

---

[1] Which they subsequently did.

would by no means appear to have lost their relish. These pieces, indeed, are not only of much greater length than, but of a very different structure from, those in the following collection, and evidently appear to have been written for the press. The popularity of the two first is evinced by their being mentioned by Laneham (or Langham), in his *Letter signifying the Queenz entertainment at Killingwoorth Castl*, 1575, along with several others, among which are some of those here printed, as extant in the whimsical but curious library of Captain Cox, a mason of Coventry, who had " great oversight in matters of storie," and appears to have been a wonderful admirer and collector of old poetry, romances, and ballads.

It is not the editor's inclination to enter more at large into the nature or merits of the poems he has here collected. The originals have fallen in his way on various occasions, and the pleasing recollection of that happiest period of which most of them were the familiar acquaintance, has induced him to give them to the public with a degree of elegance, fidelity and correctness, seldom instanced in republications of greater importance.[1] Every poem is printed from the authority refered to, with no other intentional license than was occasioned by the disuse of contractions, and a regular systematical punctuation, or became neces-

---

[1] The cuts in this edition are facsimiles of those by Bewick in the rare edition of 1791.

sary by the errors of the original, which are generally, if not uniformly, noticed in the margin, the emendation being at the same time distinguished in the text. Under these circumstances, the impression is committed to the patronage of the liberal and the candid, of those whom the artificial refinements of modern taste have not rendered totally insensible to the humble effusions of unpolished nature, and the simplicity of old times; a description of readers, it is to be hoped, sufficiently numerous to justify a wish that it may never fall into the hands of any other.

CONTENTS OF VOL. I.

I.
ADAM BEL, CLYM OF THE CLOUGHE, AND WYLLYAM OF CLOUDESLE . . . 13

II.
A MERY GESTE OF THE FRERE AND THE BOYE 41

III.
THE KING AND THE BARKER . . . 65

ADAM BEL,
CLYM OF THE CLOUGHE,
AND
WYLLYAM OF CLOUDESLE.

This very ancient, curious, and popular performance, apparently composed for the purpose of being sung in public to the harp, is extant in an old quarto, in black letter, without date, "Imprinted at London in Lothburye by Wyllyam Copland," and preserved among Mr. Garrick's Old Plays, now in the British Museum, whence it is here given. This copy was made use of by Dr. Percy, who has published the poem in his "Reliques of Ancient English Poetry,"[1] with some corrections fortunately supplied by another in his folio MS. which may possibly account for the many different readings between that publication and the present. No earlyer edition than Copland's is known. It was reprinted in 1605 by James Roberts, along with "The second part," a very inferior and servile production, of which there was, likewise, an edition in 1616, with considerable variations. Both these are in the Bodleian Library.

As there is no other memorial of these celebrated archers than the following legend, to which all the passages cited, from different authors, by the learned editor already mentioned, are evident allusions, any inquiry as to the time or reality of their existence must be little else than the sport of imagination. The passages refered to are, however, unquestionable proofs of the great popularity of the poem, which in fact has gone through numberless editions;

---

[1] *Volume I. p.* 143.

chiefly, it must be confessed, in the character of a penny-history.

The "*Englishe wood*" mentioned in v. 16, &c. is Englewood or Inglewood, an extensive forest in Cumberland, which was sixteen miles in length, and reached from Carlile to Penrith.[1] A similar observation has been already made by Dr. Percy, who adds, that "*Engle* or *Ingle-wood* signifies wood for firing." But, with submission to so good a judge, it should rather seem, in the present instance, to design a wood or forest in which extraordinary fires were made on particular occasions; a conjecture which will appear the more plausible, when it is considered that the identical spot on which Penrith beacon now stands, and where a beacon has stood for ages, was formerly within the limits of this very forest[2]; and that Ingleborough, one of "*the highest hills between Scotland and Trent,*" has obtained this name from the fires anciently lighted in the beacon erected on its flat top, where the foundation is still visible.

"*Clym of the Clough*" is properly explained by the above ingenious editor to mean Clem or Clement of the Valley. "*Cloudeslè*," of which the etymology has not been hitherto attempted, may be thought to signify *a rocky pasture*; from clud, rupes, and leag, pascuum. See *Lye's Saxon Dictionary*.

---

[1] Edward the First, in hunting in this forest, is said to have killed two hundred bucks in one day. See the Additions to Cumberland, in Camden's Britannia, 1695.

[2] Ibi. and Burn's Cumberland, p. 396.

M ERY it was in grene forest,
　　Amonge the leues grene,
Wher that men walke east and west,
Wyth bowes and arrowes kene,
To ryse the dere out of theyr denne, 　　5
Such sightes hath ofte bene sene,
As by 'thre' yemen of the north countrey,
By them it is I meane:
The one of them hight Adam Bel,
The other Clym of the Clough, 　　10
The thyrd was William of Cloudesly,
An archer good ynough.
　　They were outlawed for venyson,

V. 6. as hath.　　　　*V*. 7. the.　　　　*V*. 8. as I

These yemen everechone;
They swore them brethren upon a day, 15
To Englysshewood for to gone.
Now lith and lysten, gentylmen,
That of myrthes loveth to here:
Two of them were single men,
The third had a wedded fere; 20
Wyllyam was the wedded man,
Muche more then was hys care,
He sayde to hys brethren upon a day,
To Caerlel he would fare.
For to speke with fayre Alse hys wife, 25
And with hys chyldren thre.
By my trouth, sayde Adam Bel,
Not by the counsell of me;
For if ye go to Caerlel, brother,
And from thys wylde wode wende, 30
If the justice mai you take,
Your lyfe were at an ende.
If that I come not to morowe, brother,
By pryme to you agayne,
Truste not els but that I am take, 35
Or else that I am slayne.
He toke hys leaue of hys brethren two,
And to Caerlel he is gon,
There he knocked at hys owne windowe,
Shortlye and anone. 40
Where be you, fayre Alyce my wyfe?
And my chyldren three?

V. 18. And that.   *V.* 41. your.

Lyghtly let in thyne owne husbande,
Wyllyam of Cloudesle.
Alas! then sayde fayre Alyce, 45
And syghed wonderous sore,
Thys place hath ben besette for you,
Thys half yere and more.
Now am I here, sayde Cloudesle,
I woulde that I in were;— 50
Now feche us meate and drynke ynoughe,
And let us make good chere.
She fetched hym meat and drynke plenty,
Lyke a true wedded wyfe,
And pleased hym wyth that she had, 55
Whome she loued as her lyfe.
There lay an old wyfe in that place,
A lytle besyde the fyre,
Whych Wyllyam had found of cherytye
More then seuen yere; 60
Up she rose and walked full styll,
Euel mote she spede therefoore,
For she had not set no fote on ground
In seuen yere before.
She went vnto the justice hall, 65
As fast as she could hye;
Thys nyght is come vnto this town
Wyllyam of Cloudesle.
Thereof the iustice was full fayne,
And so was the shirife also; 70
Thou shalt not trauaile hether, dame, for nought,
Thy meed thou shalt haue or thou go.

V. 50. In woulde.   *V.* 62. spende.   *V.* 71. fore.

They gaue to her a ryght good goune,
Of scarlat it was as I heard 'sayne,'
She toke the gyft and home she wente, 75
And couched her downe agayne.
They rysed the towne of mery Carlel,
In all the hast that they can,
And came thronging to Wyllyames house,
As fast as they myght gone. 80
Theyr they besette that good yeman,
Round about on euery syde,
Wyllyam hearde great noyse of folkes,
That heyther ward they hyed.
Alyce opened a 'shot' wyndow, 85
And loked all about,
She was ware of the justice and shirife bothe,
Wyth a full great route.
Alas! treason! cry'd Aleyce,
Euer wo may thou be! 90
'Go' into my chambre, my husband, she sayd,
Swete Wyllyam of Cloudesle.
He toke hys sweard and hys bucler,
Hys bow and hy[s] chyldren thre,
And went into hys strongest chamber, 95
Where he thought surest to be.
Fayre Alice folowed him as a lover true,
With a pollaxe in her hande;
He shal be dead that here cometh in
Thys dore whyle I may stand. 100

V. 74. saye. *Percy reads* Of scarlate and of graine.
V. 85. shop. *Percy reads* back window.
V. 88. great full great. *V.* 91. Gy.

Cloudeslc bent a wel good bowe,
That was of trusty tre,
He smot the justise on the brest,
That hys arrowe brest in thre.
Gods curse on his hartt, saide William, 105
Thys day thy cote dyd on,
If it had ben no better then myne,
It had gone nere thy bone.
Yelde the Cloudesle, sayd the justise,
And thy bowe and thy arrowes the fro. 110
Gods curse on hys hart, sayde fair Alce,
That my husband councelleth so.
Set fyre on the house, saide the sherife,
Syth it wyll no better be,
And brenne we therin William, he saide, 115
Hys wyfe and chyldren thre.
They fyred the house in many a place,
The fyre flew vp on hye;
Alas! then cryed fayr Alice,
I se we here shall dy. 120
William openyd hys backe wyndow,
That was in hys chambre on hye,
And wyth shetes let hys wyfe downe,
And hys chyldren thre.
Have here my treasure, sayde William, 125
My wyfe and my chyldren thre,
For Christes loue do them no harme,
But wreke you all on me.
Wyllyam shot so wonderous well,
Tyll hys arrowes were all gon, 130

V. 122. was on

And the fyre so fast vpon hym fell,
That hys bowstryng brent in two.
The spercles brent and fell hym on,
Good Wyllyam of Cloudesle!
But than wax he a wofull man,   135
And sayde, thys is a cowardes death to me.
Leuer I had, sayde Wyllyam,
With my sworde in the route to renne,
Then here among myne ennemyes wode,
Thus cruelly to bren.   140
He toke hys sweard and hys buckler,
And among them all he ran,
Where the people were most in prece,
He smot downe many a man.
There myght no man stand hys stroke,   145
So fersly on them he ran;
Then they threw wyndowes and dores on him,
And so toke that good yeman.
There they hym bounde both hand and fote,
And in depe dongeon hym cast;   150
Now, Cloudesle, sayd the hye justice,
Thou shalt be hanged in hast.
One vow shall I make, sayde the sherife,
A payre of new galowes shal I for the make,
And the gates of Caerlel shal be shutte,   155
There shall no man come in therat.
Then shall not helpe Clim of the Cloughe,
Nor yet shall Adam Bell,
Though they came with a thousand mo,
Nor all the deuels in hell.   160
Early in the mornyng the justice vprose,
To the gates first gan he gon,

And commaundede to be shut full cloce
Lightile everychone.
Then went he to the market place,   165
As fast as he coulde hye,
A payre of new gallous there dyd he vp set,
Besyde the pyllory.
A lytle boy stod them amonge,
And asked what meaned that gallow tre ;   170
They sayde, to hange a good yeaman,
Called Wyllyam of Cloudesle.
That lytle boye was the towne swyne heard,
And kept 'fayre' Alyce swyne,
Oft he had seene Cloudesle in the wodde,   175
And geuen hym there to dyne.
He went out att a creues in the wall,
And lightly to the wood dyd gone,
There met he with these wight yonge men,
Shortly and anone.   180
Alas! then sayde that lytle boye,
Ye tary here all to longe ;
Cloudesle is taken and dampned to death,
All readye for to honge.
Alas! then sayde good Adam Bell,   185
That ever we see thys daye!
He myght her with vs have dwelled,
So ofte as we dyd him praye!
He myght have taryed in grene foreste,
Under the shadowes sheene,   190
And have kepte both hym and vs in reaste,
Out of trouble and teene!

V: 174. there.

Adam bent a ryght good bow,
A great hart sone had he slayne,
Take that, chylde, he sayde to thy dynner, 195
And bryng me myne arrowe agayne.
Now go we hence, sayed these wight yong men,
Tary we no lenger here;
We shall hym borowe, by gods grace,
Though we bye it full dere.   200
To Caerlel went these good yemen,
On a mery mornyng of Maye.
Here is a fyt of Cloudesli,
And another is for to saye.

[THE SECOND FIT.]

AND when they came to mery Caerlell,
   In a fayre mornyng tyde,   206
They founde the gates shut them vntyll,
Round about on euery syde.
Alas! than sayd good Adam Bell,
That euer we were made men!   210
These gates be shut so wonderous wel,
That we may not come here in.
Then spake him Clym of the Clough,
Wyth a wyle we wyl vs in bryng;
Let vs saye we be messengers,   215
Streyght come nowe from our king.

V. 201. Cyerlel.

Adam said, I haue a letter written wel,
Now let us wysely werke,
We wyl saye we haue the kinges seales,
I holde the portter no clerke.   220
Then Adam Bell bete on the gate,
With strokes great and strong,
The porter herde such noyse therat,
And to the gate he throng.
Who is there nowe, sayde the porter,   225
That maketh all thys knocking?
We be tow messengers, sayde Clim of the Clough,
Be come ryght from our kyng.
We haue a letter, sayd Adam Bel,
To the justice we must it bryng;   230
Let vs in our messag to do,
That we were agayne to our kyng.
Here commeth none in, sayd the porter,
By hym that dyed vpon a tre,
Tyll a false thefe be hanged,   235
Called Wyllyam of Cloudesle.
Then spake the good yeman Clym of the Clough,
And swore by Mary fre,
And if that we stande longe wythout,
Lyke a thefe hanged shalt thou be.   240
Lo here we haue the kynges seale;
What! lordeyne, art thou wode?
The porter went it had ben so,
And lyghtly dyd of hys hode.
Welcome be my lordes seale, he saide,   245
For that ye shall come in.

V. 230. me.

He opened the gate full shortlye,
An euyl openyng for him.
Now are we in, sayde Adam Bell,
Thereof we are full faine, 250
But Christ know[s], that harowed hell,
How we shall com out agayne.
Had we the keys, said Clim of the Clough,
Ryght wel then shoulde we spede;
Then might we come out wel ynough, 255
When we se tyme and nede.
They called the porter to counsell,
And wrange hys necke in two,
And caste him in a depe dongeon,
And toke hys keys hym fro. 260
Now am I porter, sayde Adam Bel,
Se brother the keys haue we here,
The worst porter to merry Caerlel,
That ye had thys hundred yere:
And now wyll we our bowes bend, 265
Into the towne wyll we go,
For to delyuer our dere brother,
That lyueth in care and wo.
They bent theyr bowes,
And loked theyr stringes were round, 270
The market place in mery Caerlel,
They beset that stound;
And as they loked them besyde,
A paire of new galowes ther thei see,
And the justice with a quest of squyers, 275
That had judged Cloudesle there hanged to be:

V. 254. shaulde.   *V*. 275. they.

And Cloudesle hymselfe lay redy in a carte,
Fast both fote and hand,
And a stronge rop about hys necke,
All readye for to hange.   280
The justice called to him a ladde,
Cloudesle clothes should he haue,
To take the measure of that yeman,
And therafter to make hys graue.
I have seen as great a mearveile, said Cloudesli,
As betwyene thys and pryme,
He that maketh thys graue for me,
Himselfe may lye therin.
Thou speakest proudli, saide the justice,
I shall the hange with my hande :   290
Full wel herd hys brethren two,
There styll as they dyd stande.
Then Cloudesle cast hys eyen asyde,
And saw hys to brethren,
At a corner of the market place,   295
With theyr good bows bent in ther hand,
Redy the justice for to chaunce.
I se comfort, sayd Cloudesle,
Yet hope I well to fare ;
If I might haue my handes at wyll,
Ryght lytle wolde I care.   300
Then spake good Adam Bell,
To Clym of the Clough so free,
Brother, se ye marke the justyce wel,
Lo yonder ye may him see ;

V. 293. Claudesle.   V. 294. brethen.
V. 295. marked.   V. 298. will.

And at the shyr[i]fe shote I wyll, 305
Strongly with arrowe kene,
A better shote in mery Caerlel
Thys seuen yere was not sene.
They lowsed 'their' arrowes both at once,
Of no man had 'they' dread, 310
The one hyt the justice, the other the sheryfe,
That both theyr 'sides' gan blede.
All men voyded that them stode nye,
When the justice fell downe to the grounde,
And the sherife fell nyghe hym by, 315
Eyther had his deathes wounde.
All the citezens fast gan flye,
They durst no longer abyde,
They lyghtly 'then' loused Cloudesle,
Where he with ropes lay tyde. 320
Wyllyam sterte to an officer of the towne,
Hys axe out of hys hande he wronge,
On eche syde he smote them downe,
Hym thought he taryed all to long.
Wyllyam sayde to hys brethren two, 325
Thys daye let us lyue and dye,
If euer you have nede as I haue now,
The same shall you fynde by me.
They shot so well in that tyde,
For theyr stringes were of silke ful sure, 330
That they kept the stretes on euery 'side!'
That batayle dyd longe endure.
The[y] fought together as brethren tru,

V. 309. thre.   *V.* 312. sedes.   *V.* 319. they.
     V. 325. brethen.   *V.* 331. sede.

Lyke hardy men and bolde,
Many a man to the ground they thrue, 335
And many a herte made colde.
But when their arrowes were all gon,
Men preced to them full fast,
They drew theyr swordes then anone,
And theyr bowes from them cast. 340
They went lyghtlye on theyr way,
Wyth swordes and buclers round,
By that it 'was' myd of the day,
They made mani a wound.
There was an out horne in Caerlel blowen, 345
And the belles bacward did ryng;
Many a woman sayd alas!
And many theyr handes dyd wryng.
The mayre of Caerlel forth com was,
And with hym a ful great route, 350
These yemen dred him full sore,
For of theyr lyues they stode in great doute.
The mayre came armed a full great pace,
With a pollaxe in hys hande,
Many a strong man wyth him was, 355
There in that stowre to stande.
The mayre smot at Cloudlesle with his bil,
Hys bucler he brust in two,
Full many a yeman with great euyll,
Alas! treason! they cryed for wo. 360
Kepe we the gates fast they bad,
That these traytours thereout not go.
But al for nought was that the[y] wrought,

V. 336. made many a herte.   *V.* 343. mas.

For 'so' fast they downe were layde,
Tyll they all thre, that so manfulli fought, 365
Were gotten without abraide.
Haue here your keys, sayd Adam Bel,
Myne off[i]ce I here forsake,
Yf you do by my councell,
A new porter do 'ye' make. 370
He threw theyr keys at theyr heads,
And bad them euell to thryue,
And all that letteth any good yeman
To come and comfort hys wyfe.
Thus be these good yemen gon to the wod, 375
And lyghtly as 'lefe' on lynde,
The[y] lough an[d] be mery in theyr mode,
Theyr ennemyes were fer[r]e behynd.
When they came to Englyshe wode,
Under a trusty tre, 380
They found bowes full good,
And arrowes full great plentye.
So god me help, s[a]yd Adam Bell,
And Clym of the Clough so fre,
I would we were in mery Caerlel, 385
Before that fayre meyny.
They set them downe and made good chere,
And eate and drynke full well.
Here is a fet of these wyght yong men,
An other I wyll you tell. 390

V. 364. to.   *V.* 368, 369. *misplaced in the old edition.*
   V. 370. we.   *V.* 376. left.

[THE THIRD FIT.]

As they sat in Englyshe wood
    Under theyr trusty tre,
They thought they herd a woman wepe,
    But her they mought not se.
Sore then syghed the fayre Alyce,   395
And sayde, alas! that euer I sawe thys daye!
For now is my dere husband slayne,
    Alas! and wel a way!
Myght I have spoken wyth hys dere brethren,
    Or with eyther of them twayne,   400
[To let them know what him befell]
    My hart were put out of payne!
Cloudesle walked a lytle besyde,
    And loked vnder the grenewood linde,
He was ware of hys wife and chyldren thre, 405
    Full wo in hart and mynde.
Welcome wife, then sayde Wyllyam,
    Under 'this' trusti tre;
I had wende yesterday, by swete saynt John,
    Thou shulde me never 'have' se.   410
Now well is me, she sayde, that ye be here,
    My hart is out of wo.
Dame, he sayde, be mery and glad,
    And thanke my brethren two.

    V. 393. thaught.   *V*. 399, 414. brethen.
    V. 401. *supplyed from a modern edition.*
    V. 408. thus.   *V*. 410. had.

Hereof to speake, sayd Adam Bell, 415
I wis it is no bote;
The meat that we must supp withall
It runneth yet fast on fote.
Then went they down into a launde,
These noble archares all thre, 420
Eche of them slew a hart of greece,
The best they could there se.
Haue here the best, Al[y]ce my wyfe,
Sayde Wyllyam of Cloudesle,
By cause ye so bouldly stod by me, 425
When I was slayne full nye.
Then went they to supper,
Wyth suche meat as they had,
And thanked god of ther fortune,
They were both mery and glad. 430
And when they had supped well,
Certayne without any leace,
Cloudesle sayd, we wyll to our kyng,
To get vs a charter of peace;
Alce shal be at our soiournyng, 435
In a nunry here besyde,
My tow sonnes shall wyth her go,
And ther they shall abyde:
Myne eldest son shall go wyth me,
For hym haue I no care, 440
And he shall you breng worde agayn
How that we do fare.
Thus be these yemen to London gone,
As fast as they might hye,

V. 421. graece.   *V.* 427. whent.

Tyll they came to the kynges pallace, 445
Where they woulde nedes be.
And whan they came to the kynges courte,
Unto the pallace gate,
Of no man wold they aske no leave,
But boldly went in therat; 450
They preced prestly into the hall,
Of no man had they dreade,
The porter came after and dyd them call,
And with them began to chyde.
The ussher sayed, yemen, what wold ye haue?
I pray you tell me; 456
You myght thus make offycers shent:
Good syrs of whence be ye?
Syr we be out lawes of the forest,
Certayne without any leace, 460
And hether we be come to our kyng,
To get vs a charter of peace.
And whan they came before the kyng,
As it was the lawe of the lande,
The[y] kneled downe without lettyng, 465
And eche helde vp his hand.
The[y] sayed, lord we beseche the here,
That ye wyll graunt vs grace,
For we haue slaine your fat falow der,
In many a sondry place. 470
What be your nam[e]s? than said our king,
Anone that you tell me.
They sayd, Adam Bel, Clim of the Clough,
And Wyllyam of Cloudesle.
Be ye those theues, then sayd our kyng, 475
That men haue tolde of to me?

Here to god I make a vowe,
Ye shal be hanged al thre;
Ye shal be dead without mercy,
As I am kynge of this lande. 480
He commanded his officers everichone
Fast on them to lay hand.
There they toke these good yemen,
And arested them all·thre.
So may I thryue, sayd Adam Bell, 485
Thys game lyketh not me.
But, good lorde, we beseche you now,
That you graunt vs grace,
Insomuche as we be to you comen,
Or els that we may fro you passe, 490
With suche weapons as we haue here,
Till we be out of your place;
And yf we lyue this hundreth yere,
We wyll aske you no grace.
Ye speake proudly, sayd the kynge, 495
Ye shal be hanged all thre.
That were great pitye, then sayd the quene,
If any grace myght be.
My lorde, whan I came fyrst into this lande,
To be your wedded wyfe, 500
The fyrst bowne that I wold aske,
Ye would graunt it me belyfe;
And I asked neuer none tyll now,
Therefore, good lorde, graunt it me.
Now aske it, madam, sayd the kynge, 505
And graunted shall it be.
Then, good my lord, I you beseche,
These yemen graunt ye me.

Madame, ye myght have asked a bowne,
That shuld have ben worth them all thre: 510
Ye myght have asked towres and towne[s],
Parkes and forestes plenty.
None soe pleasaunt to mi pay, she said,
Nor none so lefe to me.
Madame, sith it is your desyre, 515
Your askyng graunted shal be;
But I had leuer have geuen you
Good market townes thre.
The quene was a glad woman,
And sayd, lord, gramarcy, 520
I dare undertake for them
That true men shal they be.
But, good lord, speke som mery word,
That comfort they may se.
I graunt you grace, then said our king, 525
Wasshe, felos, and to meate go ye.
They had not setten but a whyle,
Certayne without lesynge,
There came messengers out of the north,
With letters to our kyng. 530
And whan the came before the kynge,
They kneled downe vpon theyr kne,
And sayd, lord, your offycers grete you wel,
Of Caerlel in the north cuntre.
How fare my justice, sayd the kyng, 535
And my sherife also?
Syr, they be slayne, without leasynge,
And many an officer mo.
Who hath them slayne? sayd the kyng,
Anone thou tell me. 540

Adam Bel, and Clime of the Clough,
And Wyllyam of Cloudesle.
Alas! for rewth! then sayd our kynge,
My hart is wonderous sore,
I had leuer [th]an a thousand pounde, 545
I had knowne of thys before;
For I have graunted them grace,
And that forthynketh me,
But had I knowne all thys before,
They had been hanged all thre. 550
The kyng opened the letter anone,
Hymselfe he red it thro,
And founde how these thre outlawes had slaine
Thre hundred men and mo;
Fyrst the justice and the sheryfe, 555
And the mayre of Caerlel towne,
Of all the constables and catchipolles
Alyue were left not one;
The baylyes and the bedyls both,
And the sergeauntes of the law, 560
And forty fosters of the fe,
These outlawes had yslaw;
And broke his parks, and slaine his dere,
Ouer all they chose the best,
So perelous out lawes as they were, 565
Walked not by easte nor west.
When the kynge this letter had red,
In hys harte he syghed sore,
Take vp the table anone he bad,
For I may eate no more. 570
The kyng called hys best archars,
To the buttes wyth hym to go;

I wyll se these felowes shote, he sayd,
In the north haue wrought this wo.
The kynges bowmen buske them blyue, 575
And the quenes archers also,
So dyd these thre wyght yemen,
With them they thought to go.
There twyse or thryse they shote about,
For to assay they'r hande, 580
There was no shote these yemen shot,
That any prycke myght them stand.
Then spake Wyllyam of Cloudesle,
By him that for me dyed,
I hold hym neuer no good archar 585
That shuteth at buttes so wyde.
Wherat? then sayd our kyng,
I pray thee tell me.
At suche a but, syr, he sayd,
As men vse in my countree. 590
Wyllyam went into a fyeld,
And his to brethren with him,
There they set vp to hasell roddes,
Twenty score paces betwene.
I hold him an archar, said Cloudesle, 595
That yonder wande cleueth in two.
Here is none suche, sayd the kyng,
Nor none that can so do.
I shall assaye, syr, sayd Cloudesle,
Or that I farther go. 600
Cloudesly, with a bearyng arow,
Claue the wand in to.

V. 587. At what a butte now wold ye shot. *Reliques.*

Thou art the best archer, then said the king,
Forsothe that euer I se.
And yet for your loue, sayd Wylliam, 605
I wyll do more maystry:
I haue a sonne is seuen yere olde,
He is to me full deare,
I wyll hym tye to a stake,
All shall se that be here, 610
And lay an apele vpon hys head,
And go syxe score paces hym fro,
And I myselfe, with a brode arow,
Shall cleue the apple in two.
Now haste the, then sayd the kyng, 615
By   that dyed on a tre,
But yf thou do not as thou 'hast' sayde,
Hanged shalt thou be.
And thou touche his head or gowne,
In syght that men may se, 620
By all the sayntes that be in heaven,
I shall hange you all thre.
That I haue promised, said William,
I wyl it neuer forsake,
And there euen before the kynge, 625
In the earth he droue a stake,
And bound therto his eldest sonne,
And bad hym stande styll therat,
And turned the childes face fro him,
Because he shuld not sterte; 630
An apple vpon his head he set,
And then his bowe he bent,

V. 617. hest.

Syxe score paces they were out met,
And thether Cloudesle went;
There he drew out a fayr brode arrowe, 635
Hys bowe was great and longe,
He set that arrowe in his bowe,
That was both styffe and stronge;
He prayed the people that was there,
That they would styll stande, 640
For he that shooteth for such a wager,
Behoueth a stedfast hand.
Muche people prayed for Cloudesle,
That hys lyfe saued myght be,
And whan he made hym redy to shote, 645
There was many a weping eye.
Thus Cloudesle clefte the apple in two,
That many a man myght se;[1]
Ouer gods forbode, sayde the kinge,
That thou shote at me! 650
I geve the xviii. pence a day,
And my bowe shalt thou beare,
And ouer all the north countre,
I make the chyfe rydere.
And I geve the xvii. pence a day, said the quene,
By god and by my fay, 656
Come feche thy payment when thou wylt,
No man shall say the nay.
Wyllyam, I make the a gentelman,

V. 648, Percy, instead of this line, reads
His sonne he did not nee.

[1] The legend of William Tell in an English garb.

Of clothyng and of fe, 660
And thi two brethren yemen of my chambre,
For they are so semely to se;
Your sonne, for he is tendre of age,
Of my wyne seller shall he be,
And whan he commeth to mannes estate, 665
Better auaunced shall he be.
And, Wylliam, bring me your wife, said the quene,
Me longeth her sore to se,
She shal be my chefe gentelwoman,
To gouerne my nursery. 670
The yemen thanketh them full curteously,
And sayde, to some bysshop wyl we wend,
Of all the synnes that we have done
To be assoyld at his hand.
So forth be gone these good yemen, 675
As fast as they myght hye,
And after came and dwelled wyth the kynge,
And dyed good men all thre.
Thus endeth the liues of these good yemen,
God send them eternall blysse! 680
And all that with hande bowe shoteth,
That of heauen may neuer mysse!

A
MERY GESTE
OF
THE FRERE AND THE BOYE.

This well-known tale is furnished, in its present dress, by a copy in the public library of the university of Cambridge, "Enprynted at London in Flete strete at the sygne of the sonne by Wynkyn de Worde;" compared with a later edition in the Bodleian library, "Imprinted at London at the long shop adioyning vnto Saint Mildreds Church in the Pultrie by Edwarde Alde;" both in quarto and black letter, and of singular rarity, no duplicate of either being known to exist.[1] *There is, indeed, a very old, though at the same time a most vulgar and corrupted copy extant in the first of those libraries (MSS. More, Ee. 4. 35.) under the title of "The Cheylde and hes step-dame," of which, besides that almost every line exhibits a various reading, the concluding stanzas are entirely different, and have, on that account, been thought worth preserving. But the most ancient copy of all would probably have been one in the Cotton library, if the volume which contained it had not unfortunately perished, with many things of greater importance, in the dreadful fire which happened in that noble repository,* anno 1731. *Vide Smiths Catalogue, Vitellius D. XII.*

---

[1] *There was once a copy of one or other of the above editions, or some different impression, with divers other curious pieces, in the printed library of Anthony à Wood (No. 66); but the article, with others of the like nature, appears to have been clandestinely taken out.*

From the mention made in v. 429 of the city of "Orlyaunce," and the character of the "Offycyal," it may be conjectured that this poem is of French extraction; and, indeed, it is not at all improbable that the original is extant in some collection of old Fabliaux. A punishment similar to that of the good wife in this story appears to have been inflicted on the widow of a St. Gengulph, for presuming to question the reality of her husbands miracles. See Heywoods History of Women, p. 196.

The cut prefixed is an exact copy of one in the title of the most ancient edition, which, the present editor has a melancholy pleasure in reflecting, was traced for this purpose by his learned, ingenious, and valuable friend, the late John Baynes esquire.

GOD that dyed for vs all,
And dranke both eysell and gall,
Brynge vs out of bale,
And gyue them good lyfe and longe
That lysteneth to my songe, 5
Or tendeth to my tale.
There dwelled an husbonde in my countre
That had wyues thre,
By processe of tyme,
By the fyrst wyfe a sone he had, 10
That was a good sturdy ladde,
And an happy hyne.
His fader loued hym wele,
So dyde his moder neuer a dele,

I tell you as I thinke;   15
All she thought was lost, by the rode,
That dyde the lytell boye ony good,
Other mete or drynke.
And yet y wys it was but badde,
And therof not halfe ynough he had,   20
But euermore of the worste:
Therfore euyll mote she fare,
For euer she dyde the lytell boye care,
As ferforth as she dorste.
The good wyfe to her husbonde gan saye,   25
I wolde ye wolde put this boye awaye,
And that ryght soone in haste;
Truly he is a cursed ladde,
I wolde some other man hym had,
That wolde hym better chaste.   30
Then sayd the good man agayne,
Dame, I shall do the sayne,
He is but tender of age;
He shall abyde with me this yere,
Tyll he be more strongere,   35
For to wynne better wage.
We haue a man, a stoute freke,
That in the felde kepeth our nete,
Slepynge all the daye,
He shall come home, so god me shelde,   40
And the boye shall into the felde,
To kepe our beestes yf he may.
Than sayd the wyfe, verament,
Therto soone I assent,
For that me thynketh moost nedy.   45
On the morowe whan it was daye,

The lytell boye wente on his waye,
To the felde full redy;
Of no man he had no care,
But sung, hey howe, awaye the mare,[1]   50
And made ioye ynough;
Forth he wente, truly to sayne,
Tyll he came to the playne,
Hys dyner forth he drough:
Whan he sawe it was but bad,   55
Ful lytell lust therto he had,
But put it vp agayne;
Therfore he was not to wyte,
He sayd he wolde ete but lyte,
Tyll nyght that he home came,   60
And as the boye sate on a hyll,
An olde man came hym tyll,
Walkynge by the waye;
Sone, he sayde, god the se,
Syr, welcome mote ye be,   65
The lytell boye gan saye.
The olde man sayd, I am an hongred sore,
Hast thou ony mete in store,
That thou mayst gyue me?
The chyld sayd, so god me saue,   70
To such vytayle as I haue
Welcome shall ye be,

---

[1] *This seems to have been the beginning or title of some old ballad. Maystres Jyll of Brentford takes notice of it in her " Testament." 4to. b. l.*

"Ah syrra, mary a way the mare."

V. 60. came home. *De W.*

Therof the olde man was gladde,
The boye drewe forth suche as he had,
And sayd, do gladly. 75
The olde man was easy to please,
He ete and made hym well at ease,
And sayd, sone, gramercy.
Sone, thou haste gyuen mete to me,
I shall the gyue thynges thre, 80
Thou shalt them neuer forgete.
Than sayd the boye, as I trowe,
It is best that I haue a bowe,
Byrdes for to 'shete.'
A bowe, sone, I shall the gyue, 85
That shall last the all thy lyue,
And euer a lyke mete,
Shote therin whan thou good thynke,
For yf thou shote and wynke,
The prycke thow shalte hytte. 90
Whan he the bowe in honde felte,
And the boltes vnder his belte,
Lowde than he lough;
He sayd, now had I a pype,
Though it were neuer so lyte, 95
Than were I gladde ynough.
A pype, sone, thou shalte haue also,
In true musyke it shall go,
I put thee out of doubt;
All that may the pype here 100
Shall not themselfe stere,

V. 84. shote. *De W.* shoote. *A.*
V. 99. I do the well to wyte. *De W.*

But laugh and lepe aboute.
What shall the thyrde be?
For I wyll gyue the gyftes three,
As I haue sayd before.   105
The lytell boye on hym lough,
And sayd, syr, I haue ynough,
I wyll desyre no more.
The olde man sayd, my trouth I plyght,
Thou shalte haue that I the hyght;   110
Say on now and let me se.
Than sayd the boye anone,
I haue a stepdame at home,
She is a shrewe to me:
Whan my fader gyueth me mete,   115
She wolde theron that I were cheke,
And stareth me in the face;
Whan she loketh on me so,
I wolde she sholde let a rappe go,
That it myght rynge ouer all the place.   120
Than sayd the olde man tho,
Whan she loketh on the so
She shall begyn to blowe;
All that euer it may here
Shall not themselfe stere,   125
But laugh on a rowe.
Farewell, quod the olde man.
God kepe the, sayd the chylde than,
I take my leue at the;
God, that moost best may,   130
Kepe the bothe nyght and day.

V. 105. to the before. *Idem.*

Gramercy, sone, sayd he.
Than drewe it towarde the nyght,
Iacke hym hyed home full ryght,
It was his ordynaunce; 135
He toke his pype and began to blowe,
All his beestes on a rowe,
Aboute hym they can daunce.
Thus wente he pypynge thrugh the towne,
His beestes hym folowed by the sowne, 140
Into his faders close;
He wente and put them vp echone,
Homewarde he wente anone,
Into his faders hall he gose.
His fader at his souper sat, 145
Lytell Iacke espyed well that,
And sayd to hym anone,
Fader, I haue kepte your nete,
I praye you gyue me some mete,
I am an hongred, by Saynt Ihone: 150
I haue sytten metelesse
All this daye kepynge your beestes,
My dyner feble it was.
His fader toke a capons wynge,
And at the boye he gan it flynge, 155
And badde hym ete apace.
That greued his stepmoders herte sore,
As I tolde you before,
She stared hym in the face,
With that she let go a blaste, 160
That they in the hall were agaste,
It range ouer all the place.
All they laughed and had good game,

The wyfe waxed red for shame,
She wolde that she had ben gone.   165
Quod the boye, well I wote,
That gonne was well shote,
As it had ben a stone.
Cursedly she loked on hym tho,
Another blaste she let go,   170
She was almoost rente.
Quod the boye, wyll ye se
How my dame letteth pellettes fle,
In fayth or euer she stynte?
The boye sayde vnto his dame,   175
Tempre thy bombe, he sayd, for shame:
She was full of sorowe.
Dame, sayd the good man, go thy waye,
For I swere to the by my faye,
Thy gere is not to borowe.   180
Afterwarde as ye shall here,
To the hous there came a frere,
To lye there all nyght;
The wyfe loued him as a saynt,
And to hym made her complaynt,   185
And tolde hym all aryght:
Wee haue a boye within ywys,
A shrewe for the nones he is,
He dooth me moche care;
I dare not loke hym vpon,   190
I am ashamed, by Saynt Iohn,
To tell you how I fare:

V. 136. *So* A. *and* MS. all *omitted in De W.*

I praye you mete the boy tomorowe,
Bete hym well and gyue hym sorowe,
And make the boye lame.   195
Quod the frere, I shall hym bete.
Quod the wyfe, do not forgete,
He dooth me moche shame :
I trowe the boye be some wytche.
Quod the frere, I shall hym teche, 200
Haue thou no care ;
I shall hym teche yf I may.
Quod the wyfe, I the praye,
Do hym not spare.
On the morowe the boye arose,   205
Into the felde soone he gose,
His beestes for to dryue ;
The frere ranne out at the gate,
He was a ferde leest he came to late,
He ranne fast and blyue.   210
Whan he came vpon the londe,
Lytell Iacke there he fonde,
Dryuynge his beestes all alone ;
Boye, he sayd, god gyue the shame,
What hast thou done to thy dame?   215
Tell thou me anone :
But yf thou canst excuse the well,
By my trouth bete the I wyll,
I wyll no lenger abyde.
Quod the boye, what eyleth the?   220
My dame fareth as well as ye,
What nedeth ye to chyde?

V. 211. *So* A. *and* MS. a londe. *De W.*

Quod the boye, wyll ye wete
How I can a byrde shete,
And other thynge withall? 225
Syr, he sayd, though I be lyte,
Yonder byrde wyll I smyte,
And gyue her the I shall.
There sate a byrde vpon a brere,
Shote on boy, quod the frere, 230
For that me lysteth to se.
He hytte the byrde on the heed,
That she fell downe deed,
No ferder myght she flee.
The frere to the busshe wente, 235
Vp the byrde for to hente,
He thought it best for to done.
Iacke toke his pype and began to blowe,
Then the frere, as I trowe,
Began to daunce soone; 240
As soone as he the pype herd,
Lyke a wood man he fared,
He lepte and daunced aboute;
The breres scratched hym in the face,
And in many an other place, 245
That the blode brast out;
And tare his clothes by and by,
His cope and his scapelary,
And all his other wede.
He daunced amonge thornes thycke, 250
In many places they dyde hym prycke,
That fast gan he blede.
Iacke pyped and laughed amonge,
The frere amonge the thornes was thronge,

He hopped wunders hye ; 255
At the last he held vp his honde,
And sayd I haue daunced so longe,
That I am lyke to dye ;
Gentyll Iacke, holde thy pype styll,
And my trouth I plyght the tyll, 260
I will do the no woo.
Iacke sayd, in that tide,
Frere skyppe out on the ferder syde,
Lyghtly that thou were goo.
The frere out of the busshe wente, 265
All to ragged and to rente,
And torne on euery syde ;
Unnethes on hym he had one cloute,
His bely for to wrappe aboute ;
His harneys for to hyde. 270
The breres had hym scratched so in the face,
And [in] many an other place,
He was all to bledde with blode ;
All that myght the frere se,
Were fayne awaye to flee, 275
They wende he had ben wode.
Whan he came to his hoost,
Of his iourney he made no boost,
His clothes were rente all ;
Moche sorowe in his herte he had, 280
And euery man hym dradde,
Whan he came in to the hall.

V. 255.   A hoppyd wonderley hey ;
　　　　　The boy seyde, and lowhe with all,
　　　　　Thes ys a sport reyall.
　　　　　For a lord to se.　　*MS. More.*

The wyfe sayd, where hast thou bene?
In an euyll place I wene,
Me thynketh by thyn araye.   285
Dame, I haue ben with thy sone,
The deuyll of hell hym ouercome,
For no man elles may.
With that came in the good man,   290
The wife sayd to hym than,
Here is a foule araye;
Thy sone that is the lefe and dere,
Hath almoost slayne this holy frere,
Alas! and welawaye!   295
The good man sayd, *benedicite!*
What hath the boye done frere to the?
Tell me without lette.
The frere sayd, the deuyll hym spede,
He hath made me daunce, maugre my hede,
Amonge the thornes, hey go bette.[1]   301
The good man sayd to hym tho,
Haddest thou lost thy lyfe so,
It had ben grete synne.
The frere sayd, by our lady,   305
The pype went so meryly,
That I coude neuer blynne.
Whan it drewe towarde the nyght,
The boye came home full ryght,
As he was wont to do;   310
Whan he came into the hall,

---

[1] *The name, it is probable, of some old dance. To "dance hey go mad" is still a common expression in the North*

Soone his fader gan hym call,
And badde hym to come hym to.
Boye, he sayd, tell me here,
What hast thou done to the frere?   315
Tell me without lesynge.
Fader, he sayd, by my faye,
I dyde nought elles, as I you saye,
But pyped him a sprynge.
That pype, sayd his fader, wolde I here. 320
Mary, god forbede! sayd the frere;
His handes he dyde wrynge.
Yes, sayd the good man, by goddes grace.
Then, sayd the frere, out alas!
And made grete mournynge.   325
For the loue of god, quod the frere,
If ye wyll that pype here,
Bynde me to a post;
For I knowe none other rede,
And I daunce I am but deed,   330
Well I wote my lyfe is lost.
Stronge ropes they toke in honde,
The frere to the poste they bonde,
In the myddle of the halle;
All that at the souper sat   335
Laughed and had good game therat,
And said the frere wolde not fall.
Than sayd the good man,
Pype sonne, as thou can,

V. 312. His fader dyde hym soone call. *De W.*
V. 327. that he pype. *De W.*
V. 339. Pype on good sone. *Idem.*

Hardely whan thou wylle. 340
Fader, he sayd, so mote I the,
Haue ye shall ynough of gle,
Tyll ye bydde me be styll.
As soon as Iacke the pype hent,
All that there were verament, 345
Began to daunce and lepe;
Whan they gan the pype here,
They myght not themselfe stere,
But hurled on an hepe.
The good man was in no dyspayre, 350
But lyghtly lepte out of his chayre,
All with a good chere;
Some lepte ouer the stocke,
Some stombled at the blocke,
And some fell flatte in the fyre. 355
The good man had grete game,
How they daunced all in same;
The good wyfe after gan steppe,
Euermore she kest her eye at Iacke,
And fast her tayle began to cracke, 360
Lowder than they coude speke.
The frere hymselfe was almoost lost,
For knockynge his heed ayenst the post,
He had none other grace;
The rope rubbed hym vnder the chynne, 365
That the blode downe dyde rynne,
In many a dyuers place.
Iacke ranne into the strete,
After hym fast dyde they lepe,

V. 361. Lowde. *De W.*

Truly they coude not stynte; 370
They wente out at the dore so thycke,
That eche man fell on others necke,
So pretely out they wente.
Neyghbours that were fast by,
Herde the pype go so meryly, 375
They ranne into the gate;
Some lepte ouer the hatche,
They had no time to drawe the latche,
They wende they had come to late.
Some laye in theyr bedde, 380
And helde vp theyr hede,
Anone they were waked;
Some sterte in the waye,
Truly as I you saye,
Stark bely naked. 385
By that they were gadred aboute,
I wys there was a grete route,
Dauncynge in the strete;
Some were lame and myght not go,
But yet ywys they daunced to, 390
On handes and on fete.
The boye sayd, now wyll I rest.
Quod the good man, I holde it best,
With a mery chere;
Sease, sone, whan thou wylte, 395
In fayth this is the meryest fytte
That I herde this seuen yere.
They daunced all in same,
Some laughed and had good game,

V. 392. They. *W.*

And some had many a fall. 400
Thou cursed boye, quod the frere,
Here I somon the that thou appere
Before the offycyall;
Loke thou be there on Frydaye,
I wyll the mete and I may, 405
For to ordeyne the sorowe.
The boye sayd, by god auowe,
Frere, I am as redy as thou,
And Frydaye were to morowe.
Frydaye came as ye may here, 410
Iackes stepdame and the frere
Togeder there they mette;
Folke gadered a grete pase,
To here euery mannes case,
The offycyall was sette. 415
There was moche to do,
Maters more than one or two,
Both with preest and clerke;
Some had testamentes for to preue,
And fayre women, by your leue, 420
That had strokes in the derke.
Euery man put forth his case,
Then came forth frere Topyas,
And Iackes stepdame also;
Syr offycyall, sayd he, 425
I haue brought a boye to thee,
Which hath wrought me moche wo;
He is a grete nygromancere,

V. 402, 403. Y som' the affor the comserey. *MS.*
V. 423. Than cam soret capias. *MS.*

In all Orlyaunce is not his pere,
As by my trouth I trowe.   430
He is a wytche, quod the wyfe:
Than, as I shall tell you blythe,
Lowde coude she blowe.
Some laughed without fayle,
Some sayd, dame, tempre thy tayle,   435
Ye wreste it all amysse.
Dame, quod the offycyall,
Tel forth on thy tale,
Lette not for this.
The wyfe was afrayed of an other cracke,   440
That no worde more she spacke,
She durst not for drede.
The frere sayd, so mote I the,
Knaue, this is long of the
That euyl mote thou spede.   445
The frere sayd, syr offycyall,
The boye wyll combre vs all,
But yf ye may him chaste;
Syr, he hath a pype truly,
Wyll make you daunce and lepe on hye,   450
Tyll your herte braste.
The offycyall sayd, so mot I the,
That pype wolde I fayne se,

              V. 432. blyue. *A.*

V. 453,   That pype well y se,
&c.   He seyde, boy, hes het her?
        Ye scer, be mey ffay,
        Anon pype ws a lay,
        And make vs all cher.
        The offeciall the pype hent,
        And blow tell his brow hen bent,

And knowe what myrth that he can make.
Mary, god forbede, than sayd the frere,   455
That he sholde pype here,
Afore that I hens the waye take.
Pype on, Iacke, sayd the offycyall,
I wyll here now how thou canst playe.
Iacke blewe vp, the sothe to saye,   460
And made them soone to daunce all.
The offycyall lepte ouer the deske,
And daunced aboute wonder faste,
Tyll bothe his shynnes he all to brest,

Bot therof cam no gle;
The offeciall seyde, this ys nowth,
Be god that me der bowthe,
Het ys not worthe a sclo.
Be mey fay, qod the freyr,
The boy can make het pype cler,
Y bescro hem for hes mede.
The offeciall bad the boy a say.
Nay, qod the freyr, er that a way,
For that y for bede.
Pype on, qod the offeciall, and not spar.
The freyr began to star,
Jake hes pype hent,
As sone as Gake began to blow,
All they lepyd on a rowe,
And ronde abowt they went.
The offeciall had so gret hast,
That boyt hes schenys brast,
A pon a blokys hende.
The clerkys to dans they hem sped,
And som all ther eynke sched,
And som ther bekes rent,
And som cast ther boky[s] at the wall,
And som ouer ther felowys can fall,
So weytley they lepyd.
Ther was withowt let,

Hym thought it was not of the best, 465
Than cryed he vnto the chylde,
To pype no more within this place,
But to holde styll for goddes grace,
And for the loue of Mary mylde.
Than sayd Iacke to them echone, 470
If ye wolde me graunte with herte fre,
That he shall do me no vylany,
But hens to departe euen as I come.
Therto they answered all anone,
And promysed him anone ryght, 475

They stombylled on a hepe,
They dansed all a bowthe,
And yever the freyr creyd owt,
Y may no lengger dans for soyt,
Y haffe lost halffe mey cod war,
When y dansed yn the thornes.
Som to crey they began,
Mey boke ys all to toren;
Som creyd withowt let,
And som bad hoo;
Som seyde het was a god game,
And som seyde they wer lame,
Y may no leynger skeppe;
Som dansed so long,
Tell they helde owt the townge,
And a nethe meyt hepe.
The offeciall began to star,
And seyde, hafe for they heyr,
Stent of they lay,
And boldeley haske of me,
What thou welt hafe for thy gle,
Y schall the redey pay.
Then to stend Jake began,
The offeciall was a werey man,
Mey trowet y pleyt y the,
Thes was a god gle,

In his quarell for to fyght,
And defende hym from his fone,
Thus they departed in that tyde,
The offycyall and the sompnere,
His stepdame and the frere,
With great ioye and moche pryde.   480

And seyde the worst that euer they se,
For het was er neyth.
Then bespake the offeciall,
And leytley Gake can call,
Hes pype he hem hent,
And gaffe hem xx s.
And euer mor hes blesyng,
For that merey set.
When Gake had that money hent,
Anon homard he went,
Glad therof was he ;
He waxed a wordeley marchande,
A man of gret degre.
Hes stepdame, y dar say,
Dorst neuer after that day,
Nat wonley ones desplese.
They lowyd togedyr all thre,
Hes father, hes stepdame and he,
Affter yn gret eys.
And that they ded, soyt to say,
Tho hewyn they tooke the way,
Withowtyn eney mes.
Now god that dyed for os all,
And dranke aysell and gall,
Bryng them all to they bles,
That beleuet on the name Jhc.

THE KING

AND

THE BARKER.

The following equally rude and ancient piece is given from the manuscript volume in the public library, Cambridge, already described. It is the undoubted original of "the merry, pleasant, and delectable history between K. Edward the fourth and a tanner of Tamworth," reprinted by Dr. Percy; who ought, perhaps, to have informed his readers that the old copies contain a great many stanzas which he has, not injudiciously, suppressed.

Dantre is Daventry (vulgarly pronounced Daintry), in Warwickshire.

The writer of the manuscript should seem to have been some provincial rustic. In one place of the volume he enters the following saw, which appeared worth preserving, for the sake of its singularity.

 Ther ys leythe reythe and meythe,
 Meythe ouerset reythe for the defawte of leythe,
 Bot and reythe methe com to leythe,
 Scholder neuer meythe ouerset reythe.

WELL yow her a god borde to make yow
'all lawhe?'
How het fell apon a tyme, or eney man het know,
The kyng rod a hontyng as that tyme was,
For to hont a der y trow hes hope was.
As he rode he houertoke yn the wey   5
A tannar of Dantre yn a queynte a raye;
Blake kow heydys sat he apon,
The hornys heyng besyde,
The kyng low and had god game,
To se the tannar reyde.   10
Howr kyng bad hes men abeyde,
And he welde sper of hem the wey;

V. 1. lawhe all.

Yffe y may her eney new tythyng
Y schall het to yow saye.
Howr kyng prekyd, and seyde, ser, god and saffe. 15
The tannar seyde, well mot yow ffar.
God felow, seyde 'howr' kyng, off on thyng y the
  pray,
To Drayton Baset well y reyde, wyche ys the wey?
That can y tell the fro hens that y stonde,
When thow comest to the galow tre torne vpon the
  lyft honde. 20
Gramercy, felow, seyde owr kyng, withowtyn eney
  'wone,'
I schall prey they lord Baset thanke the sone.
God felow, seyde owr kyng, reyde thou with me,
Tell y com to Drayton Baset, now y het se.
Nay be 'mey feyt' seyde the barker thoo, 25
Thow may sey y wer a fole and y dyd so;
I hast yn mey wey as well as thow hast yn theyne,
Reyde forthe and seke they wey, thi hors ys better
  nar meyne.
The tannar seyde, what maner man ar ye?
A preker abowt, seyd the kyng, yn maney a contre. 30
Than spake the thanner, foll scredely ayen,
Y had a brother vowsed the same
Tull he cowde never the.
Than 'howr' kyng smotley gan smeyle,
Y prey the felow reyde with me a meyle. 35
What devell, quod the tannar, art thou owt off they
  wet?

  V. 13. now. *V.* 17. yowr.
 V. 21. woyt. *V.* 25. meyt. *V.* 34. yowr.

Y most hom to mey deyner, for I am fastyng yet.
Good felow, seyde owr kyng, car the not for no mete,
Thou schalt haffe mete ynow to neyzt, and yeffe thou welt ette.
The tanner toke gret skorne of hem, 40
And swar be creyst ys pyne,
Y trow y hafe mor money in mey pors
Nar thow hast yn theyne :
Wenest thow y well be owt on neyzt? nay, and god be for,
Was y neuer owt a neyt sen y was bor. 45
The tanner lokyd a bake tho,
The heydes began to fall,
He was war of the keyngs men,
Wher they cam reydyng all.
Thes ys a theffe, thowt the tanner, 50
Y prey to god geffe hem car,
He well haffe mey hors,
Mey heydes, and all mey chaffar.
For feleyschepe, seyde the tannar,
Yet wel y reyde with the ; 55
Y not war y methe with the afterward
Thow mast do as meche for me.
God a mar[sey], seyde owr kyng, withowt eny wone,
Y schall prey the lord Baset to thanke the sone.
Owr keyng seyde, what new tydyng herest as thou ryd ? 60
I wolde fayne wet for thow reydest weyde.

V. 60. now.

Y know now teytheyng, the thanner seyde, kerhe
    and thou schalt here,
Off al the chaffar that y know kow heydys beyt der.
Owr keyng seyde, on theyng, as mey loffe y the prey,
What herest sey be the lord Baset yn thes contrey? 65
I know hem not, seyde the tanner, with hem y hafe
    lytyll to don,
Wolde he neuer bey of me clot lether to clowt 'his
    schoyn.'
Howr kyng seyde, y loffe the well, of on thyng y
    the praye,
Thow hast harde hes servants speke, what welde
    they saye?
Ye for god, seyde the tanner, that tell y can,   70
Thay sey thay leke hem well, for he ys a god man.
Thos they reyd together talkyng, for soyt y yow
    tell,
Tull he met the lord Baset, on kneys downe they fell.
Alas, the thanner thowt, the kyng ylone thes be,
Y schall be hongyd, well y wot, at men may me se. 75
He had no meynde of hes hode, nor cape ner adell,
Al for drede off hes leyffe he wende to halfe ler.
The thanner wolde astole awey,
Whyle he began to speke,
Howr kyng had yever an ey on hem,   80
That he meyt not skape.
God felow, with me thow most abeyde, seyd owr
    kyng,
For thow and y most an hontyng reyde.

V. 67. with schoys.

Whan they com to Kyng chas meche game they saye.
Howr kyng seyde, felow what schall y do, my hors
 ys so hey? 85
God felow, lend thow me theyne, and hafe her
 meyne.
Tho the tannar leyt done, and cast a downe hes
 heydys ;
Howr kyng was yn hes sadell, no leyngger he
 beydes.
Alas, theyn the thanner thowt, he well reyde away
 with mey hors,
Y well after to get hem and y may. 90
He welde not leffe hes heydys beheynde for
 notheyng,
He cast them yn the kyngs schadyll, that was a
 neys seyte ;
Tho he sat aboffe them, as y ouw saye,
He prekyd fast after hem and fond the redey wey.
The hors lokyd abowt hem, and sey on euery
 seyde 95
The kow hornes blake and wheyte ;
The hors went he had bor the deuell on hes bake ;
The hors prekyd as he was wode,
Het mestoret to spor hem not ;
The barker cleynt on hem fast, 100
He was for a ferde for to fall,
The kyng lowhe, and was glad to folow the chas,
'Yette' he was agast lest the tanner welde ber hem
 downe.

V. 103. Yeffe.

The hors sped hem sweythyli, he sped hem wonder-
  ley fast,
Ayen a bow of a noke the thanneres had he barst, 105
With a stombellyng as he rode the thanner downe
  he cast ;
The kyng lowhe, and had god game, and seyde
  thou reydyst to fast.
The kyng lowhe, and had god game, and swar be
  sent John,
Seche another horsman say y neuer none.
Owr kyng lowhe, and had god bord, and swar be
  sent 'Jame,' 110
Y most nedyst lawhe and thow wer mey dame.
Y be scro the same son, seyde the barker tho,
That seche a bord welde haffe to se hes dame so
  wo.
When 'ther' hontyng was ydo, they changyd hors
  agen,
Tho the barker had hes howyn, theyrof he was
  'fayne.' 115
Godamarsey, seyd our kyng, of they serueyse to
  daye,
Yeffe thow hafe awt to do with me, or owt to
  saye,
They frende schall y yeffor be, be god that vs bet
  on.
Godamarsey, seyde the barker tho, thow semyst a
  felow god,
Yeffe y met the yn Dantre thou schalt dreynke be
  [the] rode. 120

V. 110. Jane.   *V.* 114. her.   *V.* 115. of fayne.

Be mey feyt, seyde owr kyng, or els wer y to blame;
Yeff y met the yn Lecheffelde thou schalt hafe the same.
Thus they rod talkyng togeder to Drayton hall,
Tho the barker toke hes leffe of the lordes all.
Owr kyng comand the barker yn that tyde, 125
A C. s.[1] yn hes pors to mend hes kow heydys.
Ther owr kyng and the barker partyd feyr a twyn
God that set yn heffen so hey breyng os owt of sen!

---
[1] *i e* 100 shillings.

Hazell, Watson, & Viney, Limited, London and Aylesbury.

[**Collectanea Adamantæa.**]

PIECES OF
ANCIENT POPULAR POETRY.

Of this edition only 75 large-paper and 275 small-paper copies are printed for subscribers.

COLLECTANEA ADAMANTÆA.—VI.

Ancient Popular Poetry:

FROM

AUTHENTIC MANUSCRIPTS

AND

OLD PRINTED COPIES.

Edited by
JOSEPH RITSON,

AND

Revised by
EDMUND GOLDSMID, F.R.H.S.

ADORNED WITH CUTS.

VOL. II.

PRIVATELY PRINTED.
EDINBURGH.
1884.

Hazell, Watson, & Viney, Limited, London and Aylesbury.

CONTENTS OF VOL. II.

I.
                                                                    Page
HOW A MERCHANDE DYD HIS WYFE BE-
TRAY   1

II.
HOW THE WISE MAN TAUGHT HIS SON .   13

III.
THE LIFE AND DEATH OF TOM THUMBE .   23

IV.
THE LOVERS' QUARREL: OR, CUPID'S
TRIUMPH   42

GLOSSARY   63

HOW A MERCHANDE DYD HYS WYFE BETRAY.

The story of this ancient poem seems to have appeared in all possible shapes. It is contained in a tract intitled "Penny-wise, pound-foolish; or a Bristow diamond, set in two rings, and both crack'd. Profitable for married men, pleasant for young men, and a rare example for all good women," London, 1631. 4to. b.l. and is well known, at least in the North, by the old ballad called "The Pennyworth of Wit." It likewise appears, from Langham's Letter, 1575, to have been then in print, under the title of "The Chapman of a Pennyworth of Wit;" though no edition of that age is now known to exist. The following copy is from a transcript made by the late Mr. Baynes from one of Bp. More's manuscripts in the public library at Cambridge (Ff. 2. 38, or 690), written apparently about the reign of Edward the fourth or Richard the third; carefully but unnecessarily examined with the original. The poem itself however is indisputably of a greater age, and seems from the language and orthography to be of Scotish, or at least of North country extraction. The fragment of a somewhat different copy, in the same dialect, is contained in a MS. of Henry the 6ths time in the British Museum (Bib. Har. 5396). It has evidently been designed to be sung to the harp.

L YSTENYTH, lordyngys, y you pray,
How a merchand dyd hys wyfe betray,
Bothe be day and be nyght,
Yf ye wyll herkyn aryght.
Thys songe ys of a merchand of thys cuntre, 5
That had a wyfe feyre and free;
The marchand had a full gode wyfe,
Sche louyd hym trewly as hur lyfe,
What that euyr he to hur sayde,
Euyr sche helde hur wele apayde: 10
The marchand, that was so gay,
By another woman he lay;

He boght hur gownys of grete pryce,
Furryd with menyvere and with gryse,
To hur hedd ryall atyre, 15
As any lady myght desyre ;
Hys wyfe, that was so trewe as ston,
He wolde ware no thyng vpon :
That was foly be my fay,
That fayrenes schulde tru loue betray. 20
So hyt happenyd, as he wolde,
The marchand ouer the see he schulde ;
To hys leman ys he gon,
Leue at hur for to tane ;
With clyppyng and with kyssyng swete, 25
When they schulde parte bothe dyd they wepe.
Tyll hys wyfe ys he gon,
Leue at her then hath he tan ;
Dame, he seyde, be goddys are,
Haste any money thou woldyst ware ? 30
Whan y come bezonde the see
That y myzt the bye some ryche drewrè.
Syr, sche seyde, as Cryst me saue,
Ye haue all that euyr y haue ;
Ye schall haue a peny here, 35
As ye ar my trewe fere,
Bye ye me a penyworth of wytt,
And in youre hert kepe wele hyt.
Styll stode the merchand tho,
Lothe he was the peny to forgoo, 40
Certen sothe, as y yow say,
He put hyt in hys purce and yede hys way.
A full gode wynde god hath hym sende,
Yn Fraunce hyt can hym brynge ;

A full gode schypp arrayed he   45
Wyth marchaundyce and spycerè.
Certen sothe, or he wolde reste,
He boght hys lemman of the beste,
He boght hur bedys, brochys and ryngys,
Nowchys of golde, and many feyre thyngys;
He boght hur perry to hur hedd,   51
Of safurs and of rubyes redd ;
Hys wyfe, that was so trew as ston,
He wolde ware nothyng vpon :
That was foly be my fay,   55
That fayrenes schulde trew loue betray.
When he had boght all that he wolde,
The marchand ouyr the see he schulde.
The marchandys man to hys mayster dyd speke,
Oure dameys peny let vs not forgete.   60
The marchand swore, be seynt Anne,
Zyt was that a lewde bargan,
To bye owre dame a penyworth of wytt,
In all Fraunce y can not fynde hyt.
'An' olde man in the halle stode,   65
The marchandys speche he undurzode ;
The olde man to the marchand can say,
A worde of counsell y yow pray,
And y schall selle yow a penyworth of wyt,
Yf ye take gode hede to hyt :   70
Tell me marchand, be thy lyfe,
Whethyr haste thou a leman or a wyfe ?
Syr, y haue bothe, as haue y reste,
But my paramour loue I beste.

V. 65. And.

Then seyde the olde man, withowten were, 75
Do now as y teche the here ;
When thou comyst ouyr the salte fome,
Olde clothys then do the vpon,
To thy lemman that thou goo,
And telle hur of all thy woo ; 80
Syke sore, do as y the say,
And telle hur all thy gode ys loste away,
Thy schyp ys drownyd in the fom,
And all thy god ys loste the from ;
When thou haste tolde hur soo, 85
Then to thy weddyd wyfe thou go ;
Whedyr helpyth the bettur yn thy nede,
Dwelle with hur, as Cryste the spede.
The marchand seyde, wele must thou fare,
Have here thy peny, y haue my ware. 90
When he come ouer the salte fome,
Olde clothys he dyd hym vpon,
Hys lemman lokyd forthe and on hym see,
And seyde to hur maydyn, how lykyth the ?
My love ys comyn fro beyonde the see, 95
Come hedur, and see hym wyth thyn eye.
The maydyn seyde, be my fay,
He ys yn a febull array.
Go down, maydyn, in to the halle,
Yf thou mete the marchand wythalle, 100
And yf he spyrre aftyr me,
Say, thou sawe me wyth non eye ;
Yf he wyll algatys wytt,
Say in my chaumbyr y lye sore syke,

V. V. 79, 80. *These two lines are in the MS. inserted after the four following.*

Out of hyt y may not wynne, 105
To speke wyth none ende of my kynne,
Nother wyth hym nor wyth none other,
Thowe he were myn own brother.
Allas! seyde the maydyn, why sey ye soo?
Thynke how he helpyed yow owt of moche wo.
Fyrst when ye mett, wyth owt lesynge, 111
Youre gode was not worthe xx s.,
Now hyt ys worthe cccc pownde,
Of golde and syluyr that ys rounde;
Gode ys but a lante lone, 115
Some tyme men haue hyt, and some tyme none;
Thogh all hys gode be gon hym froo,
Neuyr forsake hym in hys woo.
Go downe, maydyn, as y bydd the,
Thou schalt no lenger ellys dwelle wyth me.
The maydyn wente in to the halle, 121
There sche met the marchand wythall.
Where ys my lemman? where ys sche?
Why wyll sche not come speke wyth me?
Syr, y do the wele to wytt, 125
Yn hyr chaumbyr sche lyeth full syke,
Out of hyt sche may not wynne,
To speke wyth non ende of hur kynne,
Nother wyth yow nor wyth non other,
Thowe ye were hur owne brother. 130
Maydyn, to my lemman that thou go,
And telle hur my gode ys loste me fro,
My schyp ys drownyd in the fom,
And all my gode ys loste me from;
A gentylman have y slawe, 135
Y dar not abyde the londys lawe;

Pray hur, as sche louyth me dere,
As y have ben to hur a trewe fere,
To kepe me preuy in hur chaumbyr,
That the kyngys baylyes take me neuyr.   140
Into the chaumbyr the maydyn ys goon,
Thys tale sche told hur dame anone.
In to the halle, maydyn, wynde thou downe,
And bydd hym owt of my halle to goon,
Or y schall send in to the towne,   145
And make the kyngys baylyes to come;
Y swere, be god of grete renown,
Y wyll neuyr harbur the kyngys feloun.
The maydyn wente in to the halle,
And thus sche tolde the merchand alle;   150
The marchand sawe none other spede,
He toke hys leve and forthe he yede.
Lystenyth, lordyngys, curtes and hende,
For zyt ys the better fytt behynde.

[THE SECOND FIT.]

LYSTENYTH, lordyngys, great and small:
The marchand ys now to hys own halle;
Of hys comyng hys wyfe was fayne,
Anone sche come hym agayne.
Husbonde, sche seyde, welcome ye be,
How haue ye farde beyonde the see?   160
Dame, he seyde, be goddys are,
All full febyll hath be my fare;
All the gode that euer was thyn and myn
Hyt ys loste be seynt Martyn;

In a storme y was bestadde, 165
Was y neuyr halfe so sore adrad,
Y thanke hyt god, for so y may,
That euyr y skapyd on lyve away;
My schyp ys drownyd in the fom,
And all my gode ys loste me from; 170
A gentylman haue y slawe,
I may not abyde the londys lawe;
I pray the, as thou louest me dere,
As thou art my trewe weddyd fere,
In thy chaumber thou woldest kepe me dern.
Syr, sche seyde, no man schall me warne: 176
Be stylle, husbonde, sygh not so sore,
He that hathe thy gode may sende the more;
Thowe all thy gode be fro the goo,
I wyll neuyr forsake the in thy woo; 180
Y schall go to the kyng and to the quene,
And knele before them on my kneen,
There to knele and neuyr to cese,
Tyl of the kyng y haue getyn thy pees:
I can bake, brewe, carde and spynne, 185
My maydenys and y can sylvyr wynne,
Euyr whyll y am thy wyfe,
To maynten the a trewe mannys lyfe.
Certen sothe, as y yow say,
All nyght be hys wyfe he lay, 190
On the morne, or he forthe yede,
He kaste on hym a ryall wede,
And bestrode a full gode stede,
And to hys lemmans hows he yede.
Hys lemman lokyd forthe and on hym see, 195
As he come rydyng ouyr the lee,

Sche put on hur a garment of palle,
And mett the marchand in the halle,
Twyes or thryes, or euyr he wyste,
Trewly sche had hym kyste. 200
Syr, sche seyde, be seynt John,
Ye were neuyr halfe so welcome home.
Sche was a schrewe, as haue y hele,
There sche currayed fauell well.
Dame, he seyde, be seynt John, 205
Zyt ar not we at oon;
Hyt was tolde me beyonde the see,
Thou haste another leman then me,
All the gode that was thyn and myne,
Thou haste geuyn hym, be seynt Martyn. 210
Syr, as Cryste bryng me fro bale,
Sche lyeth falsely that tolde the that tale;
Hyt was thy wyfe, that olde trate,
That neuyr gode worde by me spake;
Were sche dedd (god lene hyt wolde!) 215
Of the haue all my wylle y schulde;
Erly, late, lowde and stylle,
Of the schulde y haue all my wylle:
Ye schall see, so muste y the,
That sche lyeth falsely on me. 220
Sche leyde a canvas on the flore,
Longe and large, styffe and store,
Sche leyde theron, wythowten lyte,
Fyfty schetys waschen whyte,
Pecys of syluyr, masers of golde; 225
The marchand stode hyt to be holde:
He put hyt in a wyde sakk,
And leyde hyt on the hors bakk;

He bad hys chylde go belyue,
And lede thys home to my wyue. 230
The chylde on hys way ys gon,
The marchande come aftyr anon ;
He caste the pakk downe in the flore,
Longe and large, styf and store,
As hyt lay on the grounde, 235
Hyt was wele worthe cccc pownde :
They on dedyn the mouth aryght,
There they sawe a ryall syght.
Syr, sayde hys wyfe, be the rode,
Where had ye all thys ryall gode ? 240
Dame, he seyde, be goddys are,
Here ys thy penyworth of ware ;
Yf thou thynke hyt not wele besett,
Gyf hyt another can be ware hytt bett ;
All thys wyth thy peny boght y, 245
And therfore y gyf hyt the frely ;
Do wyth all what so euyr ye lyste,
I wyll neuyr aske yow accowntys, be Cryste.
The marchandys wyfe to hym can say,
Why come ye home in so febull array ? 250
Then seyde the marchand, sone ageyn,
Wyfe, for to assay the in certeyn ;
For at my lemman was y before,
And sche by me sett lytyll store,
And sche louyd bettyr my gode then me, 255
And so wyfe dydd neuyr ye.
To tell hys wyfe then he began,
All that gode he had takyn fro hys lemman ;
And all was becawse of thy peny,
Therfore y gyf hyt the frely ; 260

And y gyf god a vowe thys howre,
Y wyll neuyr more have paramowre,
But the, myn own derlyng and wyfe,
Wyth the wyll y lede my lyfe.
Thus the marchandys care be gan to kele, 265
He lefte hys folye euery dele,
And leuyd in clennefse and honestè;
Y pray god that so do we.
God that ys of grete renowne,
Saue all the gode folke of thys towne : 270
Jesu, as thou art heuyn kynge,
To the blys of heuyn owre soules brynge.

HOW THE WISE MAN TAUGHT HIS SON.

This little moral piece, which, for the time wherein it was written, is not inelegant, is given from a manuscript collection in the Harleian library in the British Museum (No. 1596), compiled in the reign of King Henry the sixth. It is not supposed to have been before printed, nor has any other copy of it been met with in manuscript; there is however a striking coincidence of idea in Mr. Gilbert Coopers beautiful elegy intitled "A father's advice to his son," as well as in the old song of "It's good to be merry and wise;" which the more curious reader may consult at his leisure.

L YSTENYTH all, and ze well here
    How the wyse man taght hys son ;
Take gode tent to thys matere,
    And fond to lere yf the con.
Thys song be zonge men was begon,   5
    To make hem tyrsty and stedfast ;
But zarn that is oft tyme yll sponne,
    Euyll hyt comys out at the last.

A wyse man had a fayre chyld,
    Was well of fyftene zere age,   10
That was bothe meke and mylde,
    Fayre of body and uesage ;
Gentyll of kynde and of corage,
    For he schulde be hys fadur eyre ;

Hys fadur thus, yn hys langage, 15
   'Taght' hys sone bothe weyll and fayre :

And sayd, son, kepe thys word yn hart,
   And thenke theron 'tyll' thou be ded ;
Zeyr day thy furst weke,
   Loke thys be don yn ylke stede : 20
Furst se thye god yn forme of brede,*
   And serue hym 'well' for hys godenes,
And afturward, sone, by my rede,
   Go do thy worldys besynes.

Forst, worschyp thy god on a day, 25
   And, sone, thys schall thou haue to 'mede,'
Skyll fully what thou pray,
   He wyll the graunt with outyn drede,
And send the al that thou hast nede,
   As 'far' as meser longyyth to strech, 30
This lyfe in mesur that thou lede,
   And of the remlant thou ne rech.

And, sone, thy tong thou kepe also,
   And be not tale wyse be no way,
Thyn owen tonge may be thy fo, 35
   Therfor beware, sone, j the pray,
Where and when, son, thou schalt say,
   And be whom thou spekyst oght ;
For thou may speke a word to day
   That seuen zere thens may be forthozt. 40

V. 16. That.   *V.* 18. thyll.   *V.* 22. wyll.
V. 26. mad.   *V.* 30. for.
* i. e. *go to mass.*

Therefore, sone, be ware be tyme,
  Desyre no offys for to bere,
For of thy neyborys mawgref,
  Thou most hem bothe dysplese and dere,
Or ellys thy self thou must 'forswere,'   45
  And do not as thyn offys wolde,
And gete the mawgrefe here and there,
  More then thank a thousand fold.

And, sone, yf thou wylt lyf at ese,
  And warme among thy neyburs syt,   50
Lat newefangylnes the plese
  Oftyn to remewe nor to flyt,
For and thou do thou wantys wyt,
  For folys they remewe al to wyde;
And also, sone, an euyl 'sygne' ys hyt,   55
  A mon that can no wher abyde.

And, sone, of syche thyng j the warne,
  And on my blyssyng take gode hede,
Thou vse neuer the tauerne;
  And also dysyng j the forbede: 60
For thyse two thyngys, with outyn drede,
  And comon women, as j leue,
Maks zong men euyle to spede,
  And 'falle' yn danger and yn myschefe.

And, sone, the more gode thou hast,   65
  The rather bere the meke and lowe;
Lagh not mych for that ys wast,
  For folys ben by laghing 'knowe.'

V. 45. for swete.   *V.* 55. sagne.
V. 64. fulle.   *V.* 68. knone.

And, sone, quyte wele that thou owe,
   So that thou be of detts clere ;   70
And thus, my lefe chylde, as j 'trowe,'
   Thou mest the kepe fro davngere.

And loke thou wake not to longe,
   Ne vse not rere soperys to late ;
For, were thy complexion neuyr so strong, 75
   Wyth surfet thou mayst fordo that.
Of late walkyng oftyn debate,
   On nyztys for to syt and drynke ;
Yf thou wylt rule thyn aftate,
   Betyme go to bed and wynke.   80

And, sone, as far furth as thou may,
   On non enquest that thou come,
Nor no fals wytnesse bere away,
   Of no manys mater, all ne sum :
For better the were be defe and dowm,   85
   Then for to be on eny enquest,
That aftyr myzt be vndurnome,
   A trewe man had hys quarel lest.

And, sone, yf thou wylt haue a wyfe,
   Take hur for no couetyse,   90
But loke, sone, sche be the lefe,
   Thou wyfe bywayt and wele awyse,
That sche be gode, honest, and wyse,
   Thof sche be pore take thou no hede,
For sche 'schal' do the more seruys,   95
   Then schall a ryche with owtyn drede.

V. 71. trewe.   *V*. 95. schalt.

For better it is in rest and pes,
  A mes of potage and no more,
Than for to haue a thousand mes,
  With gret dysese and angyr sore.   100
Therfore, sone, thynk on thys lore,
  Yf thou wylt haue a wyfe with ese,
By hur gode set thou no store,
  Thoffe sche wolde the bothe feffe and sesse.

And yf thy wyfe be meke and gode,   105
  And serue the wele and 'plesantly,'
Loke that thou be not so wode,
  To charge hur then to owtragely ;
But then fare with hur esely,
  And cherysch hur for hur gode dede,   110
For thyng ouerdon vnskylfully,
  Makys wrath to grow where ys no nede.

I wyl neyther glos ne 'paynt,'
  But waran the on anodyr syde,
Yf thy wyfe come to make pleynt,   115
  On thy seruandys on any syde,
Be nott to hasty them to chyde,
  Nor wreth the or thou wytt the sothe,
For wemen yn wrethe they can not hyde,
  But sone they reyse a smokei rofe.   120

Nor, sone, be not jelows, j the pray,
  For, and thou falle in jelosye,

V. 106. plesantyl.   *V.* 113. praynt.
V. 118. *The MS. reads* wreth the not, *but the word* not *is inserted by a different, though very ancient, hand, which has corrected the poem in other places; and is certainly redundant and improper.*

Let not thy wyfe wyt in no way,
   For thou may do no more foly;
For, and thy wyfe may onys aspye   125
   That thou any thyng hur mystryst,
In dyspyte of thy fantesy,
   To do the wors ys all hur lyst.

Therfore, sone, j byd the
   Wyrche with thy wyfe as reson ys,   130
Thof sche be seruant in degre,
   In som degre she felaw ys.
Laddys that ar bundyn, so haue j blys,
   That can not rewle theyr wyves aryzt,
That makys wemen, so haue j blys,   135
   To do oftyn wrong yn plyzt.

Nor, sone, bete nott thy wyfe j rede,
   For ther yn may no help 'rise,'
Betyng may not stond yn stede,
   But rather make hur 'the to despyse:'   140
Wyth louys awe, sone, thy wyfe chastyse,
   And let fayre wordys be thy zerde;
Louys awe ys the best gyse,
   My sone, to make thy wyfe aferde.

Nor, sone, thy wyfe thou schalt not chyde,
   Nor calle hur by no vyleus name,   146
For sche that schal ly be thy syde,
   To calle hur fowle yt ys thy schame;

V 135. *The latter half of this line seems repeated by mistake.*
    V. 138. be.   *V.* 140. to despyse the.

Whan thou thyne owen wyfe wyl dyffame,
   Wele may anothyr man do so :   150
Sort and fayre men make tame
   Herte and buk and wylde roo.

And, sone, thou pay ryzt wele thy tythe*,
   And pore men of thy gode thou dele ;
And loke, sone, be thy lyfe,   155
   Thou gete thy sowle here sum hele.
Thys werld hyt turnys euyn as a whele,
   All day be day hyt wyl enpayre,
And so, sone, thys worldys wele,
   Hyt faryth but as a chery fare.   160

For all that euyr man doth here,
   Wyth besynesse and trauell bothe,
All ys wythowtyn were,
   For oure mete, drynk, and clothe ;
More getys he not, wythowtyn othe,   165
   Kyng or prynce whether that he be,
Be hym lefe, or be hym loth,
   A pore man has as mych as he.

And many a man here gadrys gode
   All hys lyfe dayes for othyr men,   170
That he may not by the rode,
   Hym self onys ete of an henne ;
But be he doluyn yn hys den,
   Anothyr schal come at hys last ende,
Schal haue hys wyf and catel then,   175
   That he has gadred another schal spende.

---

* *The author, from this and other admonitions, is supposed to have been a parson.*

Therfor, sone, be my counseyle,
   More then ynogh thou neuyr covayt,
Thou ne wost wan deth wyl the assayle,
   Thys werld ys but the fendys bayte.   180

For deth ys, sone, as I trowe,
   The most thyng that certyn ys,
And non so vncerteyn for to knowe,
   As ys the tyme of deth y wys;
And therfore so thou thynk on thys,   185
   And al that j haue seyd beforn:
And Ihesu 'bryng' vs to hys blys,
   That for us weryd the crowne of thorn.

V. 180. *The latter part of this stanza seems to be wanting.*

V. 187. brynd.

THE LIFE AND DEATH
OF
TOM THUMBE.

It is needless to mention the popularity of the following story. Every city, town, village, shop, stall, man, woman, and child, in the kingdom, can bear witness to it. Its antiquity, however, remains to be enquired into, more especially as no very ancient edition of it has been discovered. That which was made use of on the present occasion bears the following title: " Tom Thumbe, his life and death: wherein is declared many maruailous acts of manhood, full of wonder, and strange merriments. Which little knight lived in king Arthurs time, and famous in the court of Great Brittaine. London, printed for John Wright. 1630." It is a small 8vo. in black letter, was given, among many other curious pieces, by Robert Burton, author of the Anatomy of Melancholy, to the Bodleian Library (Seld. Art. L. 79.), and is the oldest copy known to be extant. There is a later edition, likewise in black letter, printed for F. Coles, and others, in Antony à Wood's collection, which has been collated, as has also a different copy, printed for some of the same proprietors, in the editor's possession. All three are ornamented with curious cuts, representing the most memorable incidents of our hero's life. They are likewise divided into chapters by short prose arguments, which, being always unnecessary, and sometimes improper, as occasioning an interruption of the narrative, are here omitted.

In Ben Jonson's Masque of the Fortunate Isles, designed for the Court, on the Twelfth Night,

1626, *Skelton, one of the characters, after mention-ing Elinor Rumming, and others, says*

> *Or you may have come*
> *In,* THOMAS THUMB,
> IN A PUDDING FAT.
> *With Doctor Rat.*

Then "The Antimasque follows: consisting of these twelve persons, Owl-glass, the four Knaves, two Ruffians, Fitz-Ale, and Vapor, Elinor Rumming, Mary Ambree, Long Meg of Westminster, TOM THUMB, *and Doctor Rat."* *

Five years before there had appeared "The History of Tom Thumbe, the Little, for his small stature surnamed, King Arthurs Dwarfe: Whose Life and aduentures containe many strange and wonderful accidents, published for the delight of merry Time-spenders. Imprinted at London for Tho: Langley, 1621, *(12mo. bl.l.)" This however was only the common metrical story turned into prose with some foolish additions by R. I. [Richard Johnson.] The Preface or Introductory Chapter is as follows, being indeed the only part of the book that deserves notice.*

"My merry Muse begets no Tales of Guy of Warwicke, nor of bould Sir Beuis of Hampton; nor will I trouble my penne with the pleasant glee of Robin Hood, little Iohn, the Fryer and his Marian; nor will I call to minde the lusty Pindar of Wakefield, nor those bold Yeomen of the North, ADAM BELL, CLEM OF THE CLOUGH, *nor* WILLIAM

---

* *Works, by Whalley,* vi. 195. "*Doctor Rat, the curate," is one of the* Dramatis Personæ *in "Gammar Gurtons Needle."*

OF CLOUDESLY, those ancient archers of all England, nor shal my story be made of the mad merry pranckes of Tom of Bethlem, Tom Lincolne, or Tom a Lin, the Diuels supposed Bastard, nor yet of Garagantua that monster of men[*], but of AN LDER TOM A TOM OF MORE ANTIQUITY, a Tom of a strange making, I meane Little Tom of Wales, no bigger then a Millers Thumbe, and therefore for his small stature, surnamed Tom Thumbe. . . . . The ANCIENT TALES of Tom Thumbe IN THE OLDE TIME, haue beene the only reuiuers of drouzy age at midnight; old and young haue with his Tales chim'd Mattens till the cocks crow in the morning; Batchelors and Maides with his Tales haue compassed the Christmas fire-blocke, till the Curfew-Bell rings candle out; the old Shepheard and the young Plow boy after their dayes labour, haue carold out a Tale of Tom Thumbe to make them merry with: and who but little Tom, hath made long nights seem short, and heauy toyles easie? Therefore (gentle Reader) considering that old modest mirth is turnd naked out of doors, while nimble wit in the great Hall sits vpon a soft cushion giuing dry bobbes; for which cause I will, if I can, new cloath him in his former liuery, and bring him againe into the Chimney Corner, where now you must imagine me to sit by a good fire,

---

[*] This is scarcely true; the titles of the two last chapters being, 1. "How Tom Thumbe riding forth to take the ayre, met with the great Garagantua, and of the speech that was betweene them." 2. "How Tom Thumbe after conference had with great Garagantua returned, and how he met with King Twadle."

amongst a company of good fellowes ouer a well spic'd Wassel-bowle of Christmas Ale telling of these merry Tales which hereafter follow." This is in the editors possession.

In the panegyric verses (by Michael Drayton and others) upon Tom Coryate and his Crudities, London, 1611, 4to. our hero is thus introduced, along with a namesake, of whom, unfortunately, we know nothing further * :

"TOM THUMBE is dumbe, vntill the pudding creepe,
" In which he was intomb'd, then out doth peepe.
" TOM PIPER is gone out, and mirth bewailes,
" He neuer will come in to tell vs tales."†

We are unable to trace our little hero above half a century further back, when we find him still popular, indeed, but, to our great mortification, in very bad company. "IN OUR CHILDHOOD (says honest Reginald Scot) our mothers maids haue so terrified vs with an ouglie diuell . . . and haue so fraied vs with bull beggers, spirits, witches, vrchens, elues, hags, fairies, satyrs, pans, faunes, sylens, kit with the cansticke, tritons, centaurs, dwarfes, giants, imps, calcars, coniurors, nymphes, chang-

---

* This is a mistake : we are all well acquainted with the old lines :
"Tom, Tom, the Piper's son,
Stole a pig, and away he run."

† In a different part of the work we find other characters mentioned, whose story is now, perhaps, irretrievably forgot:
I am not now to tell a tale
Of George a Green, or Iacke a Vale,
Or yet of Chittiface.

lings, incubus, Robin good-fellow, the spoorne, the mare, the man in the oke, the helle waine, the fieredrake, the puckle, TOM THOMBE, hob-gobblin, Tom tumbler, boncles, and such other bugs, that we are afraide of our owne shadowes." *

To these researches we shall only add the opinion of that eminent antiquary Mr. Thomas Hearne, that this History, " however looked upon as altogether fictitious, yet was CERTAINLY founded upon some AUTHENTICK HISTORY, as being nothing else, originally, but a description of KING EDGAR'S DWARF." †

---

* *Discouerie of Witchcraft.* London, 1584, 4to. *p.* 155. See also Archb. *Harsnets Declaration of Popish Impostures. Ibi.* 1604, 4to. *p.* 135.

† Benedictus Abbas, Appendix ad Præfationem, *p.* LV. *Mr. Hearne was probably led to fix upon this monarch by some ridiculous lines added, about his own time, to introduce a spurious* second *and* third *part. See the common editions of Aldermary church-yard, &c. or that intitled " Thomas Redivivus : or, a compleat history of the life and marvellous actions of Tom Thumb. In three tomes. Interspers'd with that ingenious comment of the late Dr. Wagstaff: and annotations by several hands. To which is prefix'd historical and critical remarks on the life and writings of the author."* London, 1729. FOLIO. *Dr. Wagstaff's comment was written to ridicule that of Mr. Addison, in the Spectator, upon the ballad of Chevy-Chase, and is inserted in his Works.*

IN Arthurs court Tom Thumbe did liue,
    A man of mickle might,
The best of all the table round,
    And eke a doughty knight :

His stature but an inch in height,   5
    Or quarter of a span ;
Then thinke you not this little knight,
    Was prou'd a valiant man?

His father was a plow-man plaine,
    His mother milkt the cow,   10
But yet the way to get a sonne
    'This' couple knew not how,

Untill such time this good old man
    To learned Merlin goes,
And there to him his deepe desires   15
    In secret manner showes,

How in his heart he wisht to haue
    A childe, in time to come,
To be his heire, though it might be
    No bigger than his Thumbe.   20

Of which old Merlin thus foretold,
    That he his wish should haue,
And so this sonne of stature small
    The charmer to him gaue.

No blood nor bones in him should be,   25
    In shape and being such,
That men should heare him speake, but not
    His wandring shadow touch:

But so vnseene to goe or come
    Whereas it pleasd him still;   30
Begot and borne in halfe an houre,
    To fit his fathers will:

V. 12. these.

And in foure minutes grew so fast,
  That he became so tall
As was the plowmans thumbe in height,   35
  And so they did him call

Tom Thumbe, the which the Fayry-Queene
  There gave him to his name,
Who, with her traine of Goblins grim,
  Vnto his christning came.   40

Whereas she cloath'd him richly braue,
  In garments fine and faire,
Which lasted him for many yeares
  In seemely sort to weare.

His hat made of an oaken leafe,   45
  His shirt a spiders web,
Both light and soft for those his limbes
  That were so smally bred ;

His hose and doublet thistle downe,
  Togeather weau'd full fine ;   50
His stockins of an apple greene,
  Made of the outward rine ;

His garters were two little haires,
  Pull'd from his mothers eye,
His bootes and shooes a mouses skin,   55
  There tand most curiously.

Thus, like a lustie gallant, he
  Aduentured forth to goe,
With other children in the streets
  His pretty trickes to show.   60

Where he for counters, pinns, and points,
    And cherry stones did play,
Till he amongst those gamesters young
    Had loste his stocke away.

Yet could he soone renue the same,   65
    When as most nimbly he
Would diue into 'their' cherry-baggs,
    And there 'partaker' be,

Unseene or felt by any one,
    Vntill a scholler shut   70
This nimble youth into a boxe,
    Wherein his pins he put.

Of whom to be reueng'd, he tooke
    (In mirth and pleasant game)
Black pots, and glasses, which he hung   75
    Vpon a bright sunne-beame.

The other boyes to doe the like,
    In pieces broke them quite;
For which they were most soundly whipt,
    Whereat he laught outright.   80

And so Tom Thumbe restrained was
    From these his sports and play,
And by his mother after that
    Compel'd at home to stay.

V. 67. the.   *V*. 68. a taker.

Whereas about a Christmas time,　　　85
　　His father a hog had kil'd,
And Tom 'would' see the puddings made,
　　'For fear' they should be spil'd.

He sate vpon the pudding-boule,
　　The candle for to hold ;　　　　90
Of which there is vnto this day
　　A pretty pastime told :

For Tom fell in, and could not be
　　For euer after found,
For in the blood and batter he　　　95
　　Was strangely lost and drownd.

Where searching long, but all in vaine,
　　His mother after that
Into a pudding thrust her sonne,
　　Instead of minced fat.　　　　　100

Which pudding of the largest size,
　　Into the kettle throwne,
Made all the rest to fly thereout,
　　As with a whirle-wind blowne.

For so it tumbled vp and downe,　　105
　　Within the liquor there,
As if the deuill 'had' been boyld ;
　　Such was his mothers feare,

　　V. 87. to.　　　　*V*. 88. Fear'd that.
　　　　　V. 107. had there.

That vp she tooke the pudding strait,
   And gaue it at the doore   110
Vnto a tinker, which from thence
   In his blacke budget bore.

But as the tinker climb'd a stile,
   By chance he let a cracke:
Now gip, old knaue, out cride Tom Thumbe,
   There hanging at his backe: 116

At which the tinker gan to run,
   And would no longer stay,
But cast both bag and pudding downe,
   And thence hyed fast away.   120

From which Tom Thumbe got loose at last
   And home return'd againe:
Where he from following dangers long
   In safety did remaine.

Untill such time his mother went   125
   A milking of her kine,
Where Tom vnto a thistle fast
   She linked with a twine.

A thread that helde him to the same,
   For feare the blustring winde   130
Should blow him thence, that so she might
   Her sonne in safety finde.

But marke the hap, a cow came by,
   And vp the thistle eate.
Poore Tom withall, that, as a docke,   135
   Was made the red cowes meate:

Who being mist, his mother went
  Him calling euery where,
Where art thou Tom? where art thou Tom?
  Quoth he, Here mother, here: 140

Within the red cowes belly here,
  Your sonne is swallowed vp.
The which into her feareful heart
  Most carefull dolours put.

Meane while the cowe was troubled much,
  In this her tumbling wombe,   146
And could not rest vntil that she
  Had backward cast Tom Thumbe:

Who all besmeared as he was,
  His mother tooke him vp,   150
To beare him thence, the which poore lad
  She in her pocket put.

Now after this, in sowing time,
  His father would him haue
Into the field to driue his plow,
  And therevpon him gaue   155

A whip made of a barly straw,
  To driue the cattle on:
Where, in a furrow'd land new sowne,
  Poore Tom was lost and gon.

Now by a raven of great strength   160
  Away he thence was borne,
And carried in the carrions beake
  Euen like a graine of corne,

Unto a giants castle top,
  In which he let him fall,   165
Where soone the giant swallowed vp
  His body, cloathes and all.

But in his belly did Tom Thumbe
  So great a rumbling make,
That neither day nor night he could   170
  The smallest quiet take,

Untill the gyant had him spewd
  Three miles into the sea,
Whereas a fish soone tooke him vp
  And bore him thence away.   175

Which lusty fish was after caught
  And to king Arthur sent,
Where Tom was found, and made his dwarfe,
  Whereas his dayes he spent

Long time in liuely iollity,   180
  Belou'd of all the court,
And none like Tom was then esteem'd
  Among the noble sort.

Amongst his deedes of courtship done,
  His highnesse did command,   185
That he should dance a galliard braue
  Vpon his queenes left hand.

The which he did, and for the same
  The king his signet gaue,
Which Tom about his middle wore   190
  Long time a girdle braue.

Now after this the king would not
    Abroad for pleasure goe,
But still Tom Thumbe must ride with him,
    Plac't on his saddle-bow.   195

Where on a time when as it rain'd,
    Tom Thumbe most nimbly crept
In at a button hole, where he
    Within his bosome slept.

And being neere his highnesse heart,   200
    He crau'd a wealthy boone,
A liberall gift, the which the king
    Commanded to be done,

For to relieue his fathers wants,
    And mothers, being old;   205
Which was so much of siluer coyne
    As well his armes could hold.

And so away goes lusty Tom,
    With three pence on his backe,
A heauy burthen, which might make   210
    His wearied limbes to cracke.

So trauelling two dayes and nights,
    With labour and great paine,
He came into the house whereas
    His parents did remaine;   215

Which was but halfe a mile in space
    From good king Arthurs court,
The which in eight and forty houres
    He went in weary sort.

But comming to his fathers doore,   220
  He there such entrance had
As made his parents both reioice,
  And he thereat was glad.

His mother in her apron tooke
  Her gentle sonne in haste,   225
And by the fier side, within
  A walnut shell, him plac'd:

Whereas they feasted him three dayes
  Vpon a hazell nut,
Whereon he rioted so long   230
  He them to charges put;

And there-upon grew wonderous sicke,
  Through eating too much meate,
Which was sufficient for a month
  For this great man to eate.   235

But now his businesse call'd him foorth,
  King Arthurs court to see,
Whereas no longer from the same
  He could a stranger be.

But yet a few small April drops,   240
  Which setled in the way,
His long and weary iourney forth
  Did hinder and so stay.

Until his carefull father tooke
  A birding trunke in sport,   245
And with one blast blew this his sonne
  Into king Arthurs court.

Now he with tilts and turnaments
    Was entertained so,
That all the best of Arthurs knights   250
    Did him much pleasure show.

As good Sir Lancelot of the Lake,
    Sir Tristram, and sir Guy ;
Yet none compar'd with braue Tom Thum,
    For knightly chiualry.   255

In honour of which noble day,
    And for his ladies sake,
A challenge in king Arthurs court
    Tom Thumbe did brauely make.

Gainst whom these noble knights did run,   260
    Sir Chinon, and the rest,
Yet still Tom Thumbe with matchles might
    Did beare away the best.

At last sir Lancelot of the Lake
    In manly sort came in,   265
And with this stout and hardy knight
    A battle did begin.

Which made the courtiers all agast,
    For there that valiant man
Through Lancelots steed, before them all, 270
    In nimble manner ran.

Yea horse and all, with speare and shield,
    As hardly he was seene,
But onely by king Arthurs selfe
    And his admired queene,   275

Who from her finger tooke a ring,
   Through which Tom Thumb made way,
Not touching it, in nimble sort,
   As it was done in play.

He likewise cleft the smallest haire   280
   From his faire ladies head,
Not hurting her whose euen hand
   Him lasting honors bred.

Such were his deeds and noble acts
   In Arthurs court there showne,   285
As like in all the world beside
   Was hardly seene or knowne.

Now at these sports he toyld himselfe
   That he a sicknesse tooke,
Through which all manly exercise   290
   He carelesly forsooke.

Where lying on his bed sore sicke,
   King Arthurs doctor came,
With cunning skill, by physicks art,
   To ease and cure the same.   295

His body being so slender small,
   This cunning doctor tooke
A fine prospective glasse, with which
   He did in secret looke

Into his sickened body downe,   300
   And therein saw that Death
Stood ready in his wasted guts
   To sease his vitall breath.

His armes and leggs consum'd as small
    As was a spiders web,   305
Through which his dying houre grew on,
    For all his limbes grew dead.

His face no bigger than an ants,
    Which hardly could be seene:
The losse of which renowned knight   310
    Much grieu'd the king and queene.

And so with peace and quietnesse
    He left this earth below;
And vp into the Fayry Land
    His ghost did fading goe.   315

Whereas the Fayry Queene receiu'd,
    With heauy mourning cheere,
The body of this valiant knight,
    Whom she esteem'd so deere.

For with her dancing nymphes in greene, 320
    She fetcht him from his bed,
With musicke and sweet melody,
    So soone as life was fled:

For whom king Arthur and his knights
    Full forty daies did mourne;   325
And, in remembrance of his name
    That was so strangely borne,

He built a tomb of marble gray,
    And yeare by yeare did come
To celebrate the mournefull day,   330
    And buriall of Tom Thum.

Whose fame still liues in England here,
   Amongst the countrey sort ;
Of whom our wives and children small
   Tell tales of pleasant sport.   335

THE LOVERS QUARREL:

OR,

CUPIDS TRIUMPH.

This "*pleasant History*," which "*may be sung to the tune of Floras Farewell,*" is here republished from a copy printed at London for F. Cotes and others, 1677, 12mo. bl. l. preserved in the curious and valuable collection of that excellent and most respected antiquary Antony à Wood, in the Ashmolean Museum; compared with another impression, for the same partners, without date, in the editor's possession. The reader will find a different copy of the poem, more in the ballad form, in a Collection of "*Ancient Songs,*" published by J. Johnson. Both copies are conjectured to have been modernised, by different persons, from some common original, which has hitherto eluded the vigilance of collectors, but is strongly suspected to have been the composition of an old North country minstrel.

The full title is—"*The Lovers quarrel: or Cupids Triumph: being the pleasant history of Fair Rosamond of Scotland. Being daughter to the lord Arundel, whose love was obtained by the valour of Tommy Pots: who conquered the lord Phenix, and wounded him, and after obtained her to be his wife. Being very delightful to read.*"

OF all the lords in Scotland fair,
    And ladies that been so bright of blee,
There is a noble lady among them all,
    And report of her you shall hear by me.

For of her beauty she is bright,   5
    And of her colour very fair,
She's daughter to lord Arundel,
    Approv'd his parand and his heir.

Ile see this bride, lord Phenix said,
    That lady of so bright a blee,   10
And if I like her countenance well,
    The heir of all my lands she'st be.

But when he came the lady before,
  Before this comely maid came he,
O god thee save, thou lady sweet,   15
  My heir and parand thou shalt be.

Leave off your suit, the lady said,
  As you are a lord of high degree,
You may have ladies enough at home,
  And I have a lord in mine own country ; 20

For I have a lover true of mine own,
  A serving-man of low degree,
One Tommy Pots it is his name,
  My first love, and last that ever shall be.

If that Tom Pots [it] is his name,   25
  I do ken him right verily,
I am able to spend forty pounds a week,
  Where he is not able to spend pounds three.

God give you good of your gold, she said,
  And ever god give you good of your fee, 30
Tom Pots was the first love that ever I had,
  And I do mean him the last to be.

With that lord Phenix soon was mov'd,
  Towards the lady did he threat,
He told her father, and so it was prov'd, 35
  How his daughters mind was set.

O daughter dear, thou art my own,
  The heir of all my lands to be,
Thou shalt be bride to the lord Phenix
  If that thou mean to be heir to me.

O father dear, I am your own,
   And at your command I needs must be,
But bind my body to whom you please,
   My heart, Tom Pots, shall go with thee.

Alas! the lady her fondness must leave,   45
   And all her foolish wooing lay aside,
The time is come, her friends have appointed,
   That she must be lord Phenix bride.

With that the lady began to weep,
   She knew not well then what to say,   50
How she might lord Phenix deny,
   And escape from marriage quite away.

She call'd unto her little foot-page,
   Saying, I can trust none but thee,
Go carry Tom Pots this letter fair,   55
   And bid him on Guildford-green meet me:

For I must marry against my mind,
   Or in faith well proved it shall be;
And tell to him I am loving and kind,
   And wishes him this wedding to see.   60

But see that thou note his countenance well,
   And his colour, and shew it to me;
And go thy way and high thee again,
   And forty shillings I will give thee.

For if he smile now with his lips,   65
   His stomach will give him to laugh at the [heart,
Then may I seek another true love,
   For of Tom Pots small is my part.

But if he blush now in his face,
    Then in his heart he will sorry be,   70
Then to his vow he hath some grace,
    And false to him I'le never be.

Away this lacky boy he ran,
    And a full speed forsooth went he,
Till he came to Strawberry-castle,   75
    And there Tom Pots came he to see.

He gave him the letter in his hand,
    Before that he began to read,
He told him plainly by word of mouth,
    His love was forc'd to be lord Phenix bride.   80

When he look'd on the letter fair,
    The salt tears blemished his eye,
Says, I cannot read this letter fair,
    Nor never a word to see or spy.

My little boy be to me true,   85
    Here is five marks I will give thee,
And all these words I must peruse,
    And tell my lady this from me :

By faith and troth she is my own,
    By some part of promise, so it's to be found,   90
Lord Phœnix shall not have her night nor day,
    Except he can win her with his own hand.

On Guildford-green I will her meet,
    Say that I wish her for me to pray,
For there I'le lose my life so sweet,   95
    Or else the wedding I mean to stay.

Away this lackey-boy he ran,
  Then as fast as he could hie,
The lady she met him two miles of the way,
  Says, why hast thou staid so long, my boy? 100

My little boy, thou art but young,
  It gives me at heart thou'l mock and scorn,
Ile not believe thee by word of mouth,
  Unless on this book thou wilt be sworn.

Now by this book, the boy did say, 105
  And Jesus Christ be as true to me,
Tom Pots could not read the letter fair,
  Nor never a word to spy or see.

He says, by faith and troth you are his own,
  By some part of promise, so it's to be found, 110
Lord Phenix shall not have you night nor day,
  Except he win you with his own hand.

On Guildford-green he will you meet,
  He wishes you for him to pray,
For there he'l lose his life so sweet, 115
  Or else the wedding he means to stay.

If this be true, my little boy,
  These tidings which thou tellest to me,
Forty shillings I did thee promise,
  Here is ten pounds I will give thee. 120

My maidens all, the lady said,
  That ever wish me well to prove,
Now let us all kneel down and pray,
  That Tommy Pots may win his love.

If it be his fortune the better to win, 125
    As I pray to Christ in trinity,
Ile make him the flower of all his kin,
    For the young lord Arundel he shall be.

THE SECOND PART.

LET's leave talking of this lady fair,
    In prayers full good where she may be, 130
Now let us talk of Tommy Pots,
    To his lord and master for aid went he.

But when he came lord Jockey before,
    He kneeled lowly on his knee,
What news? what news? thou Tommy Pots, 135
    Thou art so full of courtesie.

What tydings? what tydings? thou Tommy Pots,
    Thou art so full of courtesie;
Thou hast slain some of thy fellows fair,
    Or wrought to me some villany. 140

I have slain none of my fellows fair,
    Nor wrought to you no villany,
But I have a love in Scotland fair,
    And I fear I shall lose her with poverty.

If you'l not believe me by word of mouth, 145
    But read this letter, and you shall see,
Here by all these suspitious words
    That she her own self hath sent to me.

But when he had read the letter fair,
    Of all the suspitious words in it might be,   150
O Tommy Pots, take thou no care,
    Thou'st never lose her with poverty.

For thou'st have forty pounds a week,
    In gold and silver thou shalt row,
And Harvy town I will give thee,   155
    As long as thou intend'st to wooe.

Thou'st have forty of thy fellows fair,
    And forty horses to go with thee,
Forty of the best spears I have,
    And I myself in thy company.   160

I thank you, master, said Tommy Pots,
    That proffer is too good for me;
But, if Jesus Christ stand on my side,
    My own hands shall set her free.

God be with you, master, said Tommy Pots,   165
    Now Jesus Christ you save and see;
If ever I come alive again,
    Staid the wedding it shall be.

O god be your speed, thou Tommy Pots,
    Thou art well proved for a man,   170
See never a drop of blood thou spil,
    Nor yonder gentleman confound.

See that some truce with him thou take,
    And appoint a place of liberty;
Let him provide him as well as he can,   175
    As well provided thou shalt be.

But when he came to Guildford-green,
    And there had walkt a little aside,
There he was ware of lord Phenix come,
    And lady Rosamond his bride,   180

Away by the bride then Tommy Pots went,
    But never a word to her he did say,
Till he the lord Phenix came before,
    He gave him the right time of the day.

O welcome, welcome, thou Tommy Pots, 185
    Thou serving-man of low degree,
How doth thy lord and master at home,
    And all the ladies in that country?

My lord and master is in good health,
    I trust since that I did him see;   190
Will you walk with me to an out-side,
    Two or three words to talk with me?

You are a noble man, said Tom,
    And born a lord in Scotland free,
You may have ladies enough at home, 195
    And never take my love from me.

Away, away, thou Tommy Pots,
    Thou serving-man stand thou aside;
It is not a serving-man this day,
    That can hinder me of my bride.   200

If I be a serving-man, said Tom,
    And you a lord of high degree,
A spear or two with you I'le run,
    Before I'le lose her cowardly.

Appoint a place, I will thee meet, 205
   Appoint a place of liberty,
For there I'le lose my life so sweet,
   Or else my lady I'le set free.

On Guildford-green I will thee meet,
   No man nor boy shall come with me. 210
As I am a man, said Tommy Pots,
   I'le have as few in my company.

And thus staid the marriage was,
   The bride unmarried went home again,
Then to her maids fast did she laugh, 215
   And in her heart she was full fain.

My maidens all, the lady said,
   That ever wait on me this day,
Now let us all kneel down,
   And for Tommy Pots let us all pray. 220

If it be his fortune the better to win,
   As I trust to God in trinity,
Ile make him the flower of all his kin,
   For the young lord Arundel he shall be.

THE THIRD PART.

WHEN Tom Pots came home again, 225
    To try for his love he had but a week,
For sorrow, god wot, he need not care,
    For four days that he fel sick.

With that his master to him came,   [doubt,
    Says, pray thee, Tom Pots, tell me if thou
Whether thou hast gotten thy gay lady, 231
    Or thou must go thy love without.

O master, yet it is unknown,
    Within these two days well try'd it must be,
He is a lord, I am but a serving man, 235
    I fear I shall lose her with poverty.

I prethee, Tom Pots, get thee on thy feet,
    My former promises kept shall be;
As I am a lord in Scotland fair,
    Thou'st never lose her with poverty. 240

For thou'st have the half of my lands a year,
    And that will raise thee many a pound,
Before thou shalt out-braved be,
    Thou shalt drop angels with him on the ground.

I thank you, master, said Tommy Pots, 245
    Yet there is one thing of you I would fain,
If that I lose my lady sweet,
    How I'st restore your goods again?

If that thou win the lady sweet,
    Thou mayst well forth thou shalt pay me, 250
If thou loosest thy lady thou losest enough,
    Thou shalt not pay me one penny.

You have thirty horses in one close,
    You keep them all both frank and free,
Amongst them all there's an old white horse   255
    This day would set my lady free;

That is an old horse with a cut tail,
    Full sixteen years of age is he;
If thou wilt lend me that old horse,
    Then could I win her easily.   260

That's a foolish opinion, his master said,
    And a foolish opinion thou tak'st to thee;
Thou'st have a better then ever he was,
    Though forty pounds more it should cost me.

O your choice horses are wild and tough,   265
    And little they can skill of their train;
If I be out of my saddle cast,
    They are so wild they'l ne'r be tain.

Thou'st have that horse, his master said,   270
    If that one thing thou wilt me tell;
Why that horse is better then any other,
    I pray thee Tom Pots shew thou to me.

That horse is old, of stomach bold,
    And well can he skill of his train,   275
If I be out of my saddle cast,
    He'l either stand still, or turn again.

Thou'st have the horse with all my heart,
   And my plate coat of silver free,
An hundred men to stand at thy back,   280
   To fight if he thy master be.

I thank you master, said Tommy Pots,
   That proffer is too good for me,
I would not for ten thousand pounds
   Have man or boy in my company.   285

God be with you, master, said Tommy Pots,
   Now as you are a man of law,
One thing let me crave at your hand,
   Let never a one of my fellows know.

For if that my fellows they did wot,   290
   Or ken of my extremity,
Except you keep them under a lock,
   Behind me I am sure they would not be.

But when he came to Guildford-green,
   He waited hours two or three,   295
There he was ware of lord Phenix come,
   And four men in his company.

You have broken your vow, said Tommy Pots,
   The vow which you did make to me,
You said you would bring neither man nor boy,
   And now has brought more than two or three.   301

These are my men, lord Phenix said,
   Which every day do wait on me;
If any of these dare proffer to strike,
   I'le run my spear through his body.   305

I'le run no race now, said Tommy Pots,
   Except now this may be,
If either of us be slain this day,
   The other shall forgiven be.

I'le make that vow with all my heart,   310
   My men shall bear witness with me;
And if thou slay me here this day,
   In Scotland worse belov'd thou never shalt be.

They turn'd their horses thrice about,
   To run the race so eagerly;   315
Lord Phenix he was fierce and stout,
   And ran Tom Pots through the thick o' th' thigh.

He bor'd him out of the saddle fair,
   Down to the ground so sorrowfully.
For the loss of my life I do not care,   320
   But for the loss of my fair lady.

Now for the loss of my lady sweet,
   Which once I thought to have been my wife,
I pray thee, lord Phenix, ride not away,
   For with thee I would end my life.   325

Tom Pots was but a serving-man,
   But yet he was a doctor good,
He bound his handkerchief on his wound,
   And with some kind of words he stancht his blood *.

---

* i.e. *he made use of a charm for that purpose.*

He leapt into his saddle again, 330
  The blood in his body began to warm,
He mist lord Phenix body fair,
  And ran him through the brawn of the arm:

He bor'd him out of his saddle fair,
  Down to the ground most sorrowfully; 335
Says, prethee, lord Phenix, rise up and fight,
  Or yield my lady unto me.

Now for to fight I cannot tell,
  And for to fight I am not sure;
Thou hast run me throw the brawn o' the arm, 340
  That with a spear I may not endure.

Thou'st have the lady with all my heart,
  It was never likely better to prove
With me, or any nobleman else
  That would hinder a poor man of his love. 345

Seeing you say so much, said Tommy Pots,
  I will not seem your butcher to be,
But I will come and stanch your blood,
  If any thing you will give me.

As he did stanch lord Phenix blood, 350
  Lord! in his heart he did rejoice;
I'le not take the lady from you thus,
  But of her you'st have another choice.

Here is a lane of two miles long,
  At either end we set will be, 355
The lady shall stand us among,
  Her own choice shall set her free.

If thou'l do so, lord Phenix said,
  To lose her by her own choice it's honesty,
Chuse whether I get her or go her without, 360
  Forty pounds I will give thee.

But when they in that lane was set,
  The wit of a woman for to prove,
By the faith of my body, the lady said,
  Then Tom Pots must needs have his love. 365

Towards Tom Pots the lady did hie,
  To get on behind him hastily;
Nay stay, nay stay, lord Phenix said,
  Better proved it shall be.

Stay you with your maidens here, 370
  In number fair they are but three;
Tom Pots and I will go behind yonder wall,
  That one of us two be proved to dye.

But when they came behind the wall,
  The one came not the other nigh, 375
For the lord Phenix had made a vow,
  That with Tom Pots he would never fight.

O give me this choice, lord Phenix said,
  To prove whether true or false she be,
And I will go to the lady fair, 380
  And tell her Tom Pots slain is he.

When he came from behind the wall,
  With his face all bloody as it might be,
O lady sweet, thou art my own,
  For Tom Pots slain is he. 385

Now have I slain him, Tommy Pots,
    And given him deaths wounds two or three;
O lady sweet, thou art my own,
    Of all loves, wilt thou live with me?

If thou hast slain him, Tommy Pots,   390
    And given him deaths wounds two or three,
I'le sell the state of my fathers lands,
    But hanged shall lord Phenix be.

With that the lady fell in a swound,
    For a grieved woman, god wot, was she; 395
Lord Phenix he was ready then,
    To take her up so hastily.

O lady sweet, stand thou on thy feet,
    Tom Pots alive this day may be;
I'le send for thy father, lord Arundel,   400
    And he and I the wedding will see:

I'le send for thy father, lord Arundel,
    And he and I the wedding will see;
If he will not maintain you well,
    Both lands and livings you'st have of me. 405

I'le see this wedding, lord Arundel said,
    Of my daughters luck that is so fair,
Seeing the matter will be no better,
    Of all my lands Tom Pots shall be the heir.

With that the lady began for to smile,   410
    For a glad woman, god wot, was she;
Now all my maids, the lady said,
    Example you may take by me.

But all the ladies of Scotland fair,
   And lasses of England, that well would
      prove,   415
Neither marry for gold nor goods,
   Nor marry for nothing but only love :

For I had a lover true of my own,
   A serving-man of low degree ;
Now from Tom Pots I'le change his name, 420
   For the young lord Arundel he shall be.

GLOSSARY.

GLOSSARY.

Abraide, *The word. at seems to be wanting:* At a braide; *at a push; at a start. It may, however, only mean* abroad.
Adrad, *afraid.*
Algatys, *by all means.*
Among, *between.*
Amonge, *at the same time.*
And, an, *if.*
Apayde, *satisfyed, contented.*
Are, Goddys are, *Gods heir or son,* i.e. *Jesus Christ, who is also God himself.*
Array, *dress, clothing.*
Arrayed, *freighted, furnished.*
Assay, assaye, *essay, try; try, prove.*
Assoyld, *absolved.*
A twyn, *asunder.*
Auaunced, *advanced, prefered.*
Auowe, *a vow, an oath.*
Awyse.
Ayenst, *against.*
Bale, *misery, sorrow, evil.*
Bargan, *business, commission.*
Barker, *a tanner, so called from his using bark.*
Bedys, *beads.*
Belyfe, belyue, *immediately.*
Bescro, *beshrew, curse.*
Besett, *laid out, bestowed.*
Bestadde, *situated, placed.*
Bett, *better.* Ware hytt bett, *lay it out to more advantage.*
Bjl, *bill, an old English weapon, called a few lines before* "*a pollaxe.*"
Blee, *colour, complexion.*
Blynne, *stop, cease, give over.*
Blythe, blyue, *blithe, with spirit.*
Boltes, *arrows.*
Bor, *born.*
Bord, borde, *jest.*
Borowe, *bail, redeem, become pledges for.*
Bote, *boot, remedy, advantage.*

Bowne, *boon, favour.*
Braste, *burst.*
Brede, *bread.*
Bren, brenne, *burn.*
Brent, *burnt.*
Brest, *burst, broke.*
Brochys, *ornamental pins, or buckles, like the Roman fibulæ, (with a single prong) for the breast or head-dress.*
Bundyn.
Buske, *busked, addressed, prepared, got ready.*
Bywayt.
Chaste, *chastise, correct.*
Chaunce. Redy the justice for to chaunce. *This whole line seems a nonsensical interpolation.*
Cheke, *choaked.*
Chery fare.
Clennesse, *cleanness, chastity.*
Clerk, *scholar.*
Cleynt, *clung.*
Clyppyng, *embracing.*
Comand, *commanded, ordered.*
Combre, *incumber, be too many for.*
Corage, *heart, spirit, inclination, disposition.*
Curtes, *courteous.*
Dame, *mistress.* Oure dameys peny. *Our mistress's penny.*
Dampned, *condemned.*
Den, *grave.*
Dere, *hurt.*
Dern, *secret.*
Do gladly, *eat heartyly.*

Doluyn, *delved, buryed.*
Dongeon, *prison. The prison in old castles was generally under-ground.*
Dradde, *dreaded, feared.*
Drede, *fear, doubt.*
Drewrè. *The word properly signified love, courtship, &c. and hence a love-token, or love-gift; in which sense it is used by Bp. Douglas.*
Drough, *drew.*
Dyd of, *put off.*
Dyd on, *put on.*
Euerechone, everichone, euerychone, *every one.*
Eyre, *heir.*
Eysell, *vinegar.*
Fadur, *father;* his fadur eyre, *his father's heir.*
Fare, *go.*
Fauell, *deceit. See Skelton's Bowge of Courte. The meaning of the text is nevertheless still obscure, though it should seem to be the origin of our modern phrase* to curry favour.
Fay, faye, *faith.*
Fayne, *fain, glad.*
Feble, febull, febyll, *poor, wretched, miserable.*
Feche, *fetch.*
Feffe, *enfeof.*
Fere, *wife, husband, lover, friend.*
Fet, *fit, part, canto.*
Feyt, *faith.*
Flyt, *shift.*
Folys, *fools.*

GLOSSARY. 67

Fom, fome, *sea*.
Fond, *endeavour, try*.
Fone, *foes*.
Forbode, *commandment*. Ouer Gods forbode. [Præter Dei præceptum sit.] q.d. *God forbid.* (PERCY.)
Fordo, *undo, ruin, destroy*.
Forth.
Forthozt, *thought of, remembered*.
Forthynketh, *grieveth, vexeth*.
Fosters, *foresters*.
Fote, *foot*.
Found, *supported, maintained*.
Freke, *fellow*.
Froo, *from*.
Fyt, fytt, *fit, part, canto*.
Fytte, *strain*.
God, *goods, merchandize*.
Godamarsey, *a corruption of* gramercy. *See* gramarcy.
Gode, *goods, property*.
Goo, *gone*.
Goon, *go*.
Gramarcy, *thanks*, grand mercie.
Greece. Hart of Greece.
Gryse, *a species of fur*.
Gyse, *way, manner, method*.
Harowed, *ravaged, ransacked. Christ went through hell as a conqueror, and plundered it of all the souls he thought worth carrying off*.
Hatche, *a low or half door*.

Hedur, *hither*.
Hele, *health*.
Hem, *him*.
Hende, *civil, gentle*.
Hente, *take*.
Hes, *his*.
Het, *it*.
Hie, *go, run*.
High, *kye, come, hasten, return speedily*.
Hight, *was called*.
Honge, *hang, be hanged*.
Howr, *our*.
Howyn, *own*.
Hye, *go*.
Hyght, *promised*.
Hyne, *a hind is a servant*.
Kele, *cool*.
Kneen, *knees*.
Kynd, *nature*.
Lagh, *laugh*.
Laghing, *laughing*.
Lante, *lent*.
Launde, *plain, open part of a forest*.
Leace, *lyes, lying, doubt*.
Leasynge, *lying, falsehood, doubt*.
Lee, *plain, open field*.
Lefe, *agreeable*, that is the lefe, *that is so dear to thee; whom thou art so fond of, dear, or beloved.* Be hym lefe, or be hym lothe. *Let him like it or not; let him be agreeable or unwilling*.
Leffe, *leave*.
Leman, lemman, *mistress, concubine, lover, gallant, paramour*.
Lene, *lend*.

Lenger, *longer*.
Lere, *learn*.
Lesynge, *lying, falsehood*.
Lette, *delay*. Lette not for this, *be not hindered or prevented by what has happened from proceeding*.
Letteth, *let, hinder, prevent*.
Leue, *believe*.
Leuer, *rather, sooner*.
Lewde, *foolish*.
Lightile, *quickly*.
Linde, *the linden or lime tree; a tree in general*.
Lith, *incline, attend*.
Lordeyne, *fellow*. Not, as foolishly supposed, from Lord Dane, but from *lourdin* or *falourdin*, French.
Lordyngys, &c., *sirs, masters, gentlemen*.
Lore, *doctrine*.
Lough, *laugh, laughed*.
Loves. Of all loves, *an adjuration frequently used by Shakspeare and contemporary writers*.
Low, *laughed*.
Lowde and stylle, *windy and calm; foul and fair;* i.e. *in all seasons; at all times*.
Lowhe, *laughed*.
Lowsed, *let go, let fly*.
Lust, *desire, inclination*.
Lyghtly, &c., lyghtlye, *quickly, nimbly*.
Lynde. See linde.
Lyst, *inclination, desire*.

Lystenyth, *listen*.
Lyte, *little*.
Lyue, *life*.
Masers, *drinking cups*.
Maugre, *in spite of*.
Maugref, mawgrefe, *ill-will*.
Maystry. More maystry, *something in a more masterly or capital stile; a still cleverer thing*.
Mede, meed, *reward*.
Menyvere, *a sort of fur*.
Mestoret, *needed*.
Met, *meet, meted, measured*.
Metelesse, *meatless, without meat*.
Meyny, *assembly, multitude*.
Mo, *more*.
Mote, *might; may*.
Mought, *might*.
Myrthes, *pleasant passages, merry adventures*.
Nar, *nor, than*.
Nete, *cows, horned cattle*.
Neys, *nice, fine*.
Nones, *occasion*.
Nowchys of golde, *ornaments for a woman's dress; but not certain whether necklaces or hair pins*.
Nygromancere, *necromancer*.
Offycyal, &c., *the commissary or judge of a bishop's court*.
On dedyn, *undid, untyed*.
On lyue, *alive*.
Oon. Not at oon, *not at one, not friends*.

GLOSSARY.

Ordynaunce, *enjoined or regular practice.*
Other, *either.*
Out horne, *summoning horn, horn blown (as if to arms) in time of danger.*
Paramour, paramowre, *mistress, concubine.*
Parand. His parand and his heir, *his heir apparent.* My heir and parand, *my heir apparent.*
Pay, *satisfaction.*
Pees, *peace, pardon.*
Perry, *jewels, precious stones.*
Plyght, *pledge, give.*
Plyzt, *plight, condition.*
Prece, inprece, *in a press, in a crowd, in a throng.*
Preced, *pressed, thronged; pressed forward.*
Preker, *rider.*
Prekyd, *rode up; rode.*
Prestly, *readyly, quickly.*
Preue, *prove.*
Pryme, *morning;* "*The first quarter of the artificial day.*" (TYRWHITT.)
Pyne, *pain, torment.*
Quarel, *cause, suit.*
Quest, *inquest, jury.*
Quod, *quoth, said.*
Quyte, *quit, pay, discharge.*
Rech, *reck, care for.*
Rede, *advice, counsel; advise.*
Remewe, *remove.*
Renne, *run.*
Reresoperys, *after-suppers.*
Rewth, *ruth, pity.*
Rode, rood, *cross.*
Ryall, *royal, magnificent.*
Rysed, *raised, caused to rise.*
Saffe, *save.*
Safurs, *sapphires.*
Same. All in same.
Saye, *saw.*
Sayne, *say.*
Schrewe, *shrew, wicked or cursed one.*
Scredely, *shrewdly.*
Se, *seen; see, regard, superintend, keep in sight.*
Sen, *since.*
Sesse. Feffe and sesse, *enfeof and seise,* sub. *in house or land.*
Sheene.
Shent. Make officers shent, *cause them to be reprimanded.*
Shete, *shoot.*
Shot window, *a window that opens and shuts.*
Shrewe, *wicked or cursed one.*
Slawe, *slain.*
Smotley, *pleasantly.*
Sompnere, *summoner or apparitor; an officer who serves the summonses or citations of the spiritual court. See* Chaucer's Canterbury Tales.
Sothe, *truth.*
Sowne, *sound.*
Soyt, *soth, sooth, truth.*

GLOSSARY.

Sper, spyrre, *ask, enquire.*
Spercles, *sparks (of fire).*
Spycerè, *spices.*
State, *estate.*
Stere, *steer, rule, govern.*
Sterte, *started, flew.* Sterte in the waye, *started, rushed hastily, flew into the street.*
Store, *strong; value.*
Stound, *hour, time.*
Stowre, *fight.*
Stynte, *stay.*
Suspitious, *significant.*
Sweythyli, *swiftly.*
Syke, *sigh.*
Syth, *since.*
Tan, *taken.*
Tane, *take.*
Teene, *grief, sorrow.*
Tempre, *correct, manage.*
Tent, *heed.*
The, *thrive.*
Tho, *then.*
Throng, *ran.*
To, *two.*
Trate, *trot, hag.*
Trew mannys lyfe, *the life of an honest man.*
Trewe man, *honest man.*
Tyrsty, *trusty.*
Undurnome, *taken up, received, or entertained (as a notion).*
Undurzode, *understood.*
Unnethes, *scarcely.*
Verament, *truly.*
Villany, *mischief, injury.*
Vowsed.
Voyded, *avoided, withdrew, made off, got out of the way.*

Vylany, *mischief, injury.*
Vyleus, *vile, villainous, shameful.*
Waran, *warn.*
Ware, *expend, lay out.*
Ware, *purchase.*
Warne, *prevent, hinder.*
Wede, *coat, cloak, dress, attire, clothing.*
Weke. Thy furst weke, *at thy first waking; as soon as thou wakest.*
Wend, *go.*
Wende, *weened, thought.*
Were.
Wet, wete, *know.*
Wight, *strong.*
Wis, *think, take it.*
Wode, *mad.*
Wone, *hesitation.*
Wood, *mad.*
Wost, wotest, *knowest.*
Wreste, *turn.* Wreste it all amysse; *turn it the wrong way: a metaphor from tuning the harp.*
Wreth.
Wyght, *strong.*
Wyle, *feint, device, trick.*
Wynde, *wend, go.*
Wynke, *sleep.*
Wynne, *earn, get; get, come.*
Wyrche, *work, conduct thyself.*
Wys, *trow, think.*
Wyste, *knew, was aware.*
Wyt, *know.*
Wyte, *blame.*
Wytt, *know.* Do the wele to wytt, *let thee perfectly know.*

GLOSSARY.

Y, &c., *I.*
Y do, *done.*
Yede, *went.*
Yeffe, *if.*
Yeffor, *ever.*
Yong men, yonge men, *Yeomen.* *See* Spelmanni Glossarium, vv. Juniores, Yeoman.
Yslaw, *slain.*
Ywys, *I trow, I know.*
Zarn, *yarn.*
Ze, *ye.*
Zerde, *rod.*
Zere, *years.*
Zeyr day.
Zonge, *young.*
Zyt, *yet.*

www.ingramcontent.com/pod-product-compliance
Lightning Source LLC
Chambersburg PA
CBHW030343170426
43202CB00010B/1219